T0208365

Black & White

Faith

Black & White

Faith

Stories of Faith Where Gray Is Not an Option

ALISON DMYTRYSHYN-DANIELS

ARCHWAY
PUBLISHING

Copyright © 2017 Alison Dmytryshyn-Daniels.

All rights reserved. No part of this book may be used or reproduced by any means, graphic, electronic, or mechanical, including photocopying, recording, taping or by any information storage retrieval system without the written permission of the author except in the case of brief quotations embodied in critical articles and reviews.

Archway Publishing books may be ordered through booksellers or by contacting:

Archway Publishing
1663 Liberty Drive
Bloomington, IN 47403
www.archwaypublishing.com
1 (888) 242-5904

Because of the dynamic nature of the Internet, any web addresses or links contained in this book may have changed since publication and may no longer be valid. The views expressed in this work are solely those of the author and do not necessarily reflect the views of the publisher, and the publisher hereby disclaims any responsibility for them.

Any people depicted in stock imagery provided by Thinkstock are models, and such images are being used for illustrative purposes only. Certain stock imagery © Thinkstock.

Scripture taken from the New King James Version®. Copyright © 1982 by Thomas Nelson. Used by permission. All rights reserved.

ISBN: 978-1-4808-4607-4 (sc)
ISBN: 978-1-4808-4605-0 (hc)
ISBN: 978-1-4808-4606-7 (e)

Library of Congress Control Number: 2017908714

Print information available on the last page.

Archway Publishing rev. date: 7/5/2017

Contents

And they overcame him by the Blood of the
Lamb and the word of their testimony, and they
did not love their lives to the death.

—Revelation 12:11 (NKJV)

I am not a pastor of a megachurch. I do not have a degree in Bible
history or a bachelor in theology. I haven't led hundreds of thousands of people to Jesus in mass African revivals, and I haven't
written and recorded beautiful worship songs that are sung all
over the world by millions. The eyes of the masses, which are
always looking for the next big superstar, are not looking at me.

I am a forty-something average-Jane woman who goes to
work, cooks, cleans, and takes care of my family. I wear jeans and
flip-flops; ponytails are typically the extent of doing my hair, I
consume a large amount of strong black tea on a daily basis, and
there is absolutely nothing about me that would cause the world
to point their fingers at me and say, "Hey! Alison wrote a book!
We have to get that! Do you know who she *is*?" No. Not me. But I
am a woman who, when I met the real Jesus, said that I would do

whatever He asked of me, if He would fulfill His end of the bargain and make it come to fruition. I was sick to death of religious hypocrisy and was only willing to take His hand on this adventure if it meant the words of the Bible would be alive and true, not just stories that we were to read about and somehow have faith in. In 2004, my dear friend Wanda watched the miracles happen in my life and told me to write them down. She said that someday the Lord would ask me to record it all and the way He had worked in my life would inspire and heal others. I didn't listen. I thought, *Who really gives a care about what I have to say*? Over the next five years, Wanda continually said, "You need to remember to write this down!" I love you, Wanda. You're so awesome! In 2009, I started listening.

A few years went by. I met a salesman for Christian books, and he asked if I had ever thought of writing a book. I said that I had. He advised me that there was a book publishing contest going on and that I should submit my manuscript and see what happened. After laughing, I went home and thought about it. Then I prayed about it. Then I thought about it some more. *Okay*, I decided, *I'll do it!* I worked furiously to finish putting together my stories. (It would have been much easier if I had just listened to Wanda in the first place so many years before!)

Deadline looming, manuscript finished and submitted, I waited. Checked the website. Waited some more. Until the day they announced the winner, who wasn't me. Although I really didn't think I had my hopes up, I truly did. Deep down, I really had hoped that I would win and everyone would know how awesome my God was through my stories. The salesman who had told me of the contest encouraged me to continue to pursue the publishing venture. I didn't. The manuscript was shelved as the voice of doubt and disbelief told me that my stories really weren't that good and no one would really want to read them anyway. Besides, who was I that anyone would want to hear what I had to say? I am nobody. No one important. Book shelved, thoughts of publishing pushed deep down in the recesses of my mind.

Fast forward several years to present. I work full-time and do not have the privilege of participating in ministry the way that I used to. While reviewing the past year and looking forward to this new year's goals and ambitions, I asked my Lord how I could do more for the kingdom with what little time I had. "Publish the book," is what I heard. What? What book? Ooo, *that* book. I hadn't thought about it in a long time. A dream faded and dust-covered in the recesses of my memory. "Publish the book, daughter. I gave you those experiences for your benefit at the time, and now they are to benefit others."

Oh boy, publish. "Okay Lord, but I would really like a sign that this is from you before I spend thousands of dollars to do so." He is so patient with me, I know! A few days later, I was logging into my on-line school course to get set up for the next semester. The e-learning site asked each student to write a bio in the third person. If we didn't know what to write, there was a link to a website that had several great examples. Link clicked, website loaded. And there it was, the sign I had asked for. As the website finished loading, a pop-up flashed on the screen: "Are you an aspiring Christian writer? If so, click here!" Yup. That was a pretty good sign, I thought. I clicked, a salesman from this publishing house called the next day, and conversation ensued. Up to this point, I hadn't told my husband Ryan of this idea, but after speaking with the publishing house, I shared it with him. My husband is a man of few words, so when he does offer insight into something, I listen. He shared with me a video from Steve Harvey, the renowned Family Feud host. It was a mini sermon that he preached during a break on the set. He talked about how God gave each of us a gift. Whether that gift is baking or cutting grass, it can still be a gift, and if we take a chance, or a leap of faith to use that gift in our life, God would honor it. Our job is only to jump. It is about taking leaps of faith without knowing the outcome. It was now clear. A link to a publishing house on a site that I was not hunting for that information on, a husband sharing a video about taking a leap of faith, done.

I have lived the past twelve years of my life listening each day to hear God's voice and any instructions He might give me to bring the kingdom of heaven to earth. The following are some stories of how the Almighty God in heaven used his daughter to bring that kingdom down, how He healed and built up and restored things in my life that were broken, and how He grew this shy and scared woman into a warrior against the kingdom of darkness over the land. I am not a noteworthy teacher. I don't bring great insight into Bible mysteries and dive into Greek and Hebrew terminology. But I have learned that those people are few and far between. In the "in-between" are average people who have stories—stories of healings, stories of faith, stories of miracles that if told to others overcome the power of darkness in their lives and shed the light of the kingdom of heaven onto them. These are my stories. My hope is that by the blood of the Lamb and the word of my testimony or stories, you too will overcome the darkness in your world and be spurred on to seek out our awesome God in every detail of your life, whether small or large.

Acknowledgments

Utmost thanks to my Lord Jesus Christ. You created me, You watched over me, and when You knew my heart was ready to hear, You called out my name. I will be eternally thankful and grateful for my salvation, understanding that even if I were the only one on earth, You still would have left your Godship and come to earth to die on the cross—for me. I love you, my God.

Special thanks also to the following people:

My incredible husband, Ryan, and my beautiful daughters, Genevieve and Evangeline. Your sweet lives and awaiting futures inspire me to press on in making the best of everything I can so that you can have the best of everything He has for you.

My parents, Ruth and Tom Dmytryshyn. Thank you for raising me with the best you had to offer, giving me an incredible foundation and building me into the person I am today. I will be forever grateful for your love and continuous championing of me in whatever venture I pursue.

My amazing spiritual family—Bruce and Wanda Mann, where would I be without you? When I entered your church that fateful Sunday, messy and foul and unlovable, you saw past the sarcasm and the exterior hard walls and chose to love me, chose to pour your own lives into me so I could live again. You embraced me and made me as one of your own children. My thanks and gratefulness to you for all that you are. All that you have done for me will never be shelved.

Charlie and Sue Kopczyk, your missional life continues to inspire me to greater belief, greater doing. You taught me to always expect the unexpected, to ask and expect to receive, to always be obedient in whatever the Lord asks of me, for the good of His kingdom and for His glory to be renowned. Thank you for all you are and all you have done for the hundreds of thousands of people who cross WhyNot's path.

Thank you to countless great men and women of faith from the YesChurch, Highlands, and Innerkip Presbyterian Church families who taught me, encouraged me, mentored me, and spurred me on to never keep my mouth shut, even when what came out of it made you uncomfortable. Thank you for giving me the freedom to worship my Jesus and bring the kingdom of heaven to earth.

Chapter 1

He Called My Name

He came while I was lying still and prostrate on the couch with beautiful worship music playing softly and quietly in the background. As the tangible presence of my holy God entered the room, my body began to manifest His holy glory. With my spirit undone by the awesome majesty of a God indescribable, I bounced on my couch and shook in my entire being. In the midst of uncontrollable tears of reverence, my soulful mind thought, *I need to pray. I need to speak out my words of adoration. I need ...* But I was so undone that I couldn't. I began to think about the words that I wanted to say, and I lost the whole sense of His being there.

But gently, softly, He hushed me. He reminded me that my heart speaks louder than any words ever could. He showed me how Ryan and I can speak to each other without saying a word—how we can look into each other's eyes and hear every loving emotion that is stirring in each other's hearts. How we can read each other's minds without trying. How we can hear each other's voices and words without using our ears. It is the same with Him. In these intimate moments of love, there is no need for words.

I can get lost in my emotions with Him, and He can read my heart. My love speaks louder than any words ever could. And loud it was.

As I settled back down in my being, my spirit woman rose up to soar with love for my God and King. My body rocked under the emotion, and as I physically bounced uncontrollably on the couch, my heart met His in the heavens. I felt His love rush through my body like a tidal wave. He squeezed and caressed my heart. I touched His. And for a moment, I felt more love, adoration, and confirmation from Him that I was okay than ever would have happened with minutes and minutes of words spoken.

Gentle reminders came of times in the past few years when I was so overwhelmed in the world with physical trials that I didn't have any energy or drive to even utter words to Him in prayer. There were times when I had nothing left to intercede for others and when I was too tired to even formulate words. There were also times when I would do my forty-minute commute and cry all the way there in utter exhaustion, wanting to open my mouth and speak words of praise, words of intercession, or words of requests, yet I physically couldn't. But He was still there. I knew in my innermost being that even though I couldn't open my mouth to speak, even though I couldn't formulate sentences in my head to speak via thoughts, He still heard me. He knew my heart. He could read between those lines. How many times He had met me in my car. Had me pulling over to the side of the road as He met me there and wiped away my tears. Held my hand and held my heart. I didn't need to speak. I didn't need to make sentences. He didn't need them. He *knew*. He knew my thoughts, my heartaches, my desires, and my needs. He knew my everything. He knew it. And He still knows it now (Psalm 40:5).

My great God and Father has taught me that words are for others. When I am interceding for others, I speak outside my body on their behalf. The supernatural world needs to hear my words. My words are sharper than any double-edged sword, cutting through the darkness on behalf of my brothers and sisters (Hebrews 4:12). The angels of heaven are waiting at my mouth with their bowls, ready to catch my words and deliver them onto the head of the one intended (Revelation 5:8). My words are blessings or curses, and they have the ramification of such. When I am making declarations over my family, blessing them, words outside my body are required. God *spoke* the world and all creation into being. I *speak* blessings over my family, and they come to pass (Proverbs 11:11). I *intercede* out loud on behalf of my friends, family, church, and whomever the Holy Spirit brings to my mind. The words are carried supernaturally on their behalf to wherever they need to go to manifest that blessing, encouragement, or declaration. When I am in the presence of others and we are praying together, words are necessary. We encourage others by our prayers of blessing for one another. Ones who cannot formulate their prayers out loud can agree with the words spoken of others, and the two "amens" together give the words strength and weight (Matthew 18:19).

But when it's Him and me inside our secret garden, no words are required. I lie still. He meets me. As I tangibly feel His divine presence enter the room, my heart soars with adoration and love. It is uncontrollable and not manifested by any physical motivation from my soul. It just happens. Spirit woman Alison says, "Hey, my

God is here! My Father in heaven, my lover Jesus, my beautiful Holy Spirit has just come in the room! I'm coming, Jesus! I am here—I am here, right here!" Like a schoolgirl swoons when her heart's crush walks past her in the hallway, my heart swoons as He enters the room. And before I faint from just seeing His beauty, He catches me, and we embrace. And in those moments of time, everything melts away. All the troubles of the day, all the cares and concerns for my family, and all the thoughts of career and ministry are gone. All that is left is this incredible burning in my body of a love unimaginable to most—a love indescribable to others. Just love. And when those moments are past, whether they are few or many, I physically feel more relaxed and refreshed than I do after having hours of sleep. To describe it better, it's a Jello-like, melted, warm, mushy, affirmed, crazy-warm-all-the-tension-in-my-body-stripped-away-and-nothing-left-but-a-smile love.

Thank You, Lord. Thank You that You loved me enough to create me. Thank You that You loved me enough to keep me and that You loved me enough to send Jesus to die the most horrific, indescribable death to save my nonredeemable soul from an eternity of hellfire. Thank You that You love me now and that You meet me in the quiet, where it's just You and me in the four o'clock in the morning blackness. You and I twirling together in stopped time, embracing our hearts together, but for just a moment. Thank You for all You are and all You have done—and for loving me. Thank You.

A communion without bread and wine. A communion of two hearts. Four o'clock in the morning love. But this wasn't always the way my life was.

Meeting Him

"I want to get married in a church."

"What? No way."

This was the beginning of the conversation my husband and I had as we entered a building that would forever change our lives. Although we weren't Christians and I was about as disgusted with religion as any one person could possibly have been, I agreed to be married in a church because it was important to Ryan.

"Dad, I want to be a missionary. I want to go to Africa and South America and tell people about Jehovah. I want to preach the gospel and tell people about paradise. I want to change the world." Teenage talk to my dad. Hours spent in cars driving the city streets telling people about a gospel that I had been taught and believed in 100 percent. Being picked up after school and going door to door with others until six o'clock at night. Spending sixty hours per month every summer walking the sidewalks. Hundreds of hours per month for four years straight after high school knocking on doors. Putting thousands of kilometers per year on vehicles driving other Jehovah's Witnesses around as we did what we thought was right.

Yet as time went on and my desire for truth deepened, questions began arising. As I read the Bible and saw discrepancies in the translation and then questioned those discrepancies, I was told that questioning the religious authorities would lead to excommunication and that I was treading on dangerous ground if I continued. After years of being shut down in my questions and years of watching hypocrisy abound in leadership, I walked away—as far away as possible. I rebelled against everything that I had been taught, and I did exactly the opposite of everything that I had preached. I was tainted and jaded and done with religion. Many bad choices and several years later came Ryan.

The first evening we met, we sat for hours in the wan light of the moon and discussed religion. Ryan told me his stories of studying with Mormons, and I discussed the lies and false doctrines of the Witnesses. Neither of us had any interest in religion, and our lives did not reflect any kind of Christianity, but that was the topic of discussion. Two years later, when we knew we wanted to be married, the above conversation ensued. Ryan, although not able to give a reason why, was stating that it was important to him to be married in a church. I, completely uninterested in church or anything to do with it, agreed only on the sole basis that it was important to him. We thought it important to attend the church for a little bit and get to know the pastor before we asked him or her to marry us, so church-shopping we went. Three traditional old-school churches and one evangelical church later, we were ready to give up. Stale traditions, sleepy preaching, and a sea of blue hair put the traditional ones out of the question. The evangelical one? We walked out fifteen minutes into the worship as the army fatigue-clad worship leader announced, "Muslims are rising up in Toronto, and we as Christians have to fight the Muslims and take them out before they take over our country." Even our non-Christian brains knew that wasn't right, and we wanted nothing to do with it.

I was ready to quit. But the Holy Spirit had another idea. My coworker suggested that we go to the new church in town. It had been a small country congregation that had just purchased the local Ukrainian banquet hall and transformed it into a church. She had heard that it was upbeat and that they played "young charismatic" music, and she thought we might like it. Not having a clue what *charismatic* meant, I told Ryan about it, and we headed out the door the next Sunday. Little did we know that from that day forward, our lives would be changed forever.

Upon entering the doors and heading up the stairs, we knew it was different. People of every age group were smiling, talking, and laughing. The smell of coffee brewing greeted us as we entered the cafe area. Teenagers laughing with seniors. Greeters at the door who were our age and seemingly very hip. We edged our way through the crowd of hundreds of people to a back corner as the music began to play. Guitars, drums, and keyboard rocking out a fantastic tune! Teenagers leading worship with full hearts on their sleeves as they poured out their adoration for their God. And me? Snot. And tears. Ridiculous amounts of snot streaming down my face uncontrollably. What was going on? Was I allergic to something in this building? As the band played on, my sinuses unleashed the floodgates of mucus in my face, and I couldn't stop crying or stop my nose from running. The final song of the set was "Here I Am to Worship." My spiritual heart that had long been dormant was stirring. What were those words? Whom were they singing to? The little girl who had been squashed under years of bad choices and harsh religious leaders peeked her head up and out. The dried-up heart that had been so hurt and abandoned began to rehydrate under the living water that it was receiving. The bitter woman on the outside just didn't know it yet. And His voice.

Quiet. Gentle. Whispering—"Alison. Alison." I heard it. The still, quiet voice of Holy Spirit whispering to my heart, massaging my hurt, calling me home.

The following Sunday, the same thing. Great people, incredible music, excellent biblical preaching, and copious amounts of mucus from me. It was uncontrollable. As soon as the first note was strummed on the guitar, my eyes began to water. I couldn't stop myself from crying. And not just teary crying. Full-blown, I-cannot-control-this sobbing, snotting, heaving, sucking-air crying. What was going on? I had no idea. I told Ryan we had to meet the pastor and ask him to marry us so that we could stop coming here once it was done. My nose was red and raw, and I was done with this. Again, my Jesus had other plans. "Alison. Come home. Alison. I love you. I love you." *I hear you, Lord, I just don't know how to answer you right now.*

We met the pastors, and they invited us to their house the following Wednesday: "We're having a few friends over. Do you want to come?"

"Sure, why not?" We went and enjoyed random Bible discussion. They had a DVD playing in the background that was a band playing the songs that were sung on Sunday. I mentioned to the pastor's wife that I liked one of the songs, and she offered to lend me the DVD. I thought that was odd. *You don't know me, and you are offering me your DVD? You could never see me again, and you still offer it to me?* I was shocked. But still took it. Another link in the chain that led to my life being changed forever.

Two days later, I came home from work for lunch. As I sat eating my Kraft dinner and watching *The Dukes of Hazzard* reruns, the DVD drew me to itself. I could hear the songs playing, calling the little girl inside to come out and play, pulling at her heart-strings, and drawing her to the surface. I put it in and began to shake. As I scrolled through the playlist, I stopped as I saw it. "Here I Am to Worship." My heart skipped inside of me. Soul-Alison was screaming, "No, no! Don't put it in! Don't listen to it! You have to leave for work in fifteen minutes, and you know what this song does to you! Don't do it!" But Spirit-Alison, rising to the surface, took over the remote and pressed play. Seconds into the song, I watched *Him* walk in the room. Jesus came through my front door and walked into the living room. I remember seeing his glorious face but not being able to determine the features due to the light that shone from Him. Love, incredible, burning love that I had never felt before, radiated from Him. Tenderness. The tenderness of a daddy picking up his little girl who has just skinned her knee. The tenderness of a brand-new mommy kissing her newborn on the cheek for the first time. Power. The power and authority of all heaven emanating from Him. Power that is felt when a government authority walks into the room. The one-false-step-and-you-are-dead kind of power. All of this trans-pired within a second, and then I hit the floor, sobbing and weep-ing at His feet, begging Him to forgive me for all my past sins, repenting of all I had done wrong. This all within seconds as well. And as I cried out to Him, he poured His love over me. The blood shed on the cross for my sins washed over me. I felt it. I literally felt the liquid pouring over me and *washing* my ugly away. Away went the sins I had committed. Away went the black from around my heart, which kept it in bondage. Away went the hurt and the walls I had built up to protect myself. Away went the hatred for religion and the resentment that was entangled with it. He washed me clean. He made me new. There, in those few seconds on my living room floor, with worship music singing His praises in the background, I met my Jesus. I was born again. He pulled me up from the land of the dead and brought me back to the land of the living. He called my name, and I responded.

There was a man of the Pharisees named Nicodemus, a ruler of the Jews. This man came to Jesus by night and said to Him, "Rabbi, we know that You are a teacher come from God, for no one can do these signs that You do unless God is with Him."

Jesus answered and said to Him, "Most assuredly, I say to you, unless one is born again, he cannot see the kingdom of God."

Nicodemus said to Him, "How can a man be born when he is old? Can he enter a second time into his mother's womb and be born?"

Jesus answered, "Most assuredly, I say to you, unless one is born of water and the Spirit, he cannot enter the kingdom of God. That which is born of the flesh is flesh, and that which is born of the Spirit is spirit. Do not marvel that I said to you, 'you must be born again.' The wind blows where it wishes, and you hear the sound of it, but cannot tell where it comes from and where it goes. So is everyone who is born of the spirit" (John 3:1–5).

That destiny-filled day was the beginning of my new life. In our North American "Christian" society, we have become accustomed to hearing the words *saved* and *born-again*. In my old religion brain, I had no idea what that meant. I had an idea of the theory, and I had read the story of Nicodemus discussing it with Jesus, but I had never really grasped the understanding of it. I now know that my lack of understanding was because it hadn't happened to me yet. That Friday afternoon on my living room floor, the depth of what Jesus was teaching became a reality. Just as a baby is born in the natural with pain and blood, so was my new birth in the Spirit. It was Jesus's pain borne on the cross and my pain of bad life choices covered by His shed blood that birthed my new life. Little did I know how the events of that day would change my future forever: the transformations that would come to pass, the miracles I would experience, the life that I was about to lead.

Chapter 2

The Road to Health

We sat in a meeting with a Canadian guest speaker who had just returned from a mission's trip deep in the heart of Africa. He recounted story after story of miracles ranging from emotional healings to limbs growing out to the dead being raised. After a few weeks of being there, the Canadian asked the African pastor whom he was staying with why these kinds of miracles happened in Africa on a daily basis, but they didn't happen in North America. The pastor calmly answered, "Oh, that's simple. You don't believe the Bible." The Canadian missionary was flabbergasted. He told of how he stood there in disbelief that the African would dare have the audacity to say such a thing. But after moments of silence, he realized that the man was right. "They profess to know God, but in works deny Him" (Titus 1:16).

When I heard this story, I had only been a Christian a short while. But in that small window of salvation, my heart knew that this man was right. Raised in a strict religion solely focused on teaching the Word but allowing no room for belief in the Holy Spirit or His involvement in our modern world, I knew what he was talking about. I knew the verses inside out but did not comprehend their power.

From that time forward, I vowed to my God that I would believe His Word cover to cover, word for word. It would be black and white. I vowed that I would not distort the truth to fit my circumstances or make excuses when prayers weren't answered according to the promises in the Word. If my life didn't work out the way that the Gospel promised, then I would search out the reasons why. I would not rest until I moved in the miracles spoken of in Acts. I would not relent in seeking my God's face and His will for my life until I lived out and surpassed all other believers that I had heard about and read about who were moving in gifts of the Spirit. Romans says, "God is not a respecter of persons." That tells me that what He will do for one, He will do for all. We have only to ask. And if it doesn't come, then the problem is mine, not His. He promises. I just have to reach out and take it.

Plethora of Sickness

Every wedding, weekend away, special event, my mom could count on me having a cold. It never failed. Runny nose that was always red, swollen eyes, whiny voice. I was like a bad re-run. Always the never-failing cold. Growing to my six-foot stature by the age of twelve lent itself to a whole other realm of body issues. Because I felt self-conscious of my height while all other twelve-year-olds around me wavered at five feet, stooping became my norm. That led to a curving spine and nonstop aching in my back. By the time I was fourteen, the chiropractor and I were on a first-name basis. As teenagerhood came on and high school loomed, acne came to forefront, along with headaches, stomach-aches, and irritable bowel syndrome (although not yet named or society-accepted as a real illness). My body greeted the work world with additional aches and pains of monthly debilitating migraines, aches of the onset of arthritis in my wrists and knees, and symptoms of hypoglycemia. By the time I was twenty-three, my doctor diagnosed me as manic-depressive and added medication for that to my already long list. Having an aching head and an aching body was normal for me. Waking up without a headache didn't even seem like a possibility. Until one day it happened.

Within hours of meeting my Jesus, I knew something had changed. I went back to work that afternoon and told my co-worker that I had met Him. That something had changed in me. The dark cloud of evil had lifted off of my shoulders, and the world seemed brighter, literally. Within days of meeting Him, I awoke one morning and noticed that I didn't have a headache, and hadn't had one for at least two days! Within five weeks of my being born again, all symptoms of prior sickness and chronic ailments were gone. Within two months, I went back to my doctor to tell him I no longer needed anti-depressants. I told him that I had met Jesus and since then, all the hurt had disappeared. He, being medically skeptical, suggested that if I were feeling better, I should slowly wean myself off of the drugs, giving me a schedule to do so. But I knew different. I knew that the depression had been completely wiped away, and his schedule, as well as the meds, promptly found their way into the trash when I got home.

In the thirteen years that have passed since that fateful

afternoon in my living room, I have not once had a clinical headache, never mind a migraine. (Headaches now only come when I haven't eaten and immediately subside once food is ingested. Lack of food headache, not a clinical—I don't know why I have this, but it is irritating—headache.) All daily symptoms of hypoglycemia, irritable bowel syndrome, arthritis, depression? Gone. The twisted spine requiring bi-weekly visits to the chiropractor? Gone. What I read about and knew in the gospels had happened in my life. Jesus's love encountering the lost soul, and the lost soul not only being found but being made whole.

Healing of the Heart

Years passed before I realized that it wasn't just the sicknesses that Jesus took away. It wasn't a magical swoosh of His hand, a "Here, you have asked Me to be your Lord and Savior now I take away all your sickness and pain." Rather, it was "I love you, Alison. I love you. There is nothing you can say or do that will make me stop loving you. I died for you, and if you were the only person on the earth, I still would have come and died for you. Let me massage your heart. Let me heal those wounds inflicted by hurtful words and deeds of years gone by. Let me bring life back to the dead heart inside of you. Can you feel My love? Can you feel the love of heaven pouring out on you? I am the Living Water; let my water restore your soul." My Jesus gave life to my dead heart, and with that came fresh life to my dying body.

The words of the man from Africa rang in my ears every time I met a Christian who was chronically sick or who suffered with disease or illness. I would hear the words of the African pastor: "You don't believe the Bible." *Why, when I pray for these people, do they not get healed? Why do they suffer in the first place? God, your Word says that you love everyone the same, so why are all not healed as I was upon being born again?* Did I really *not* believe the Bible? It began to obsess me. Healings were all I could think about. Our church talked about healings and prayed for people to be healed, but I never saw it happen. I had read about limbs growing out and people being raised from the dead, but it only seemed to happen in third-world countries; I never heard of it happening in Canada.

Friends tipped me off to a book written by a pastor who felt the same way. He went on a sabbatical and declared a "time out" from praying for people to be healed till he found out why it wasn't happening on a regular basis. The book was *The More Excellent Way* by Pastor Henry Wright. Possessing more than four hundred pages, it was a hefty read. But I devoured it. As I read, I learned of the spiritual roots to physical sicknesses. As I scanned the index for all of the physical ailments that my body had been wrought with, I saw they all carried the same spiritual roots: self-hatred, guilt, condemnation. Bitterness, anger, and resentment. I was in shock. How could all of these physical ailments be related to what went on in my head? It wasn't what was in my head—it was in my heart. Those deep-down hurts and trials stuffed down under false smiles and pretenses. Not wanting anyone to know how much their words or behavior hurt me, I pushed it down, smiled sweetly, and convinced myself it really didn't matter. Translation: *I* really didn't matter. Translation: *I* was no good the way that I was, so I had to push down who I really was and outwardly portray who others thought I should be. *That* is what Jesus healed the day He met me. That is what he massaged out of my heart and out of my body. The love of heaven rushing through my heart healed the thirty years of prior hurts, and my body responded. As I write this, I can hear the thoughts of some who might be reading this: "Hey! I love Jesus, and I have no spiritual yuck in my heart, and I am born again, but I am still sick. Who do you think you are telling me my sickness is my fault? I'm done reading this!" If that is you, please don't put the book down. I write from my own experiences, and I write from what I have learned. But I am nowhere close to knowing it all; I am not even near the tip of the iceberg, never mind seeing the entire berg itself. Since that revelation of spiritual roots eight years ago, I have learned and re-learned that every situation is different. Every reason for a sickness is different. But there is always a reason. Whether it is a self-inflicted spiritual root, a generational curse, or a physical external environment factor, there is always a reason. But one constant remains: Jesus came to bring heaven to earth. And heaven includes whole health and a whole, perfectly healed, perfectly alive, heart. I know that I will not stop until I do what Jesus did on earth on a regular basis (John 14:12). I will not relent until every person I come in contact with sees healing from his or her sickness because of His name being spoken. Do I still get sick? On occasion. But there is always a reason. My knee swells up and aches. I know I have spoken or thought pridefully. My sinuses get filled, and I have cold and sinus infection symptoms. I am living in fear and on my own self-propulsion rather than trusting my God to sustain me and keep me. Pain comes in my girly parts. I am harboring self-hatred and guilt from listening to the condemnation of the devil. I am a work in progress, as we all are. But may the bearing of my soul inspire you to continue on, pressing forward toward the goal of life in abundance right now, right here on earth (John 10:10)!

The Long-Distance Gift

John Bevere is a world-renowned author, pastor and traveling evangelist. At a local church, we had been taking part in one of his video teaching series entitled "Extraordinary." Although it wasn't being held at our home church, we loved John's teachings and wanted to be part of it. The entire series was phenomenal. Sessions one through six discussed grace, and not just the first part of grace that we are all aware of—that it is by grace that we are saved. Grace saves us. We know that. But John discusses the other half of grace. The grace that empowers us to do what truth demands of us. The grace that, should it be engaged in our lives and asked for from God Himself, will empower us to live extraordinary lives! Lives free from sicknesses, free from condemnation, completely free as He promised!

The teaching sessions were broken down into video learning time, small group discussion time, and then small group prayer time. Our group of fifteen was made up of adults from twenty-five to sixty years old. Prior to the group coming together to discuss the video, each engaged in friendly conversation about their experiences that week, families, ailments that they were going through, upcoming surgeries, etc. Then the leader corralled the group, and textbook questions were asked, to which video-taught answers were supplied. It struck me as odd that the answers given regarding faith, healing, and prosperous living came from the same people who minutes earlier were complaining about the state their lives were in and how unhappy they were. Once the textbook answers were completed, there was no spontaneous continuation of excitement or discussion about what we had just learned. Conversation went back to complaining about their lot in life, talking of sickness running rampant through their families, including discussion of fears of cancer and other diseases. The lead pastor then requested that if everyone was finished with their textbook questions, each group was to move into a time of prayer. The leader of our group asked if anyone had any prayer requests, in response to which many asked for prayers for health, prayers for God's hands to be with the doctor for an upcoming surgery, prayers for speedy recovery, for jobs, etc. The prayers that were then voiced did not at all reflect what we had just been taught. John taught us to *appropriate* the gifts that the Father has already given us. He taught us to ask and then *receive* them from heaven, as they are sitting there waiting for us already. The prayers fell into the routine of whiny begging typical of Christians who are tired from the drudgery of religion and haven't met their real Savior yet. They profess Him as their Lord but have never appropriated His love and blessings for themselves, believing the lie that the blessings of heaven are for when we get to heaven and we just have to hold on in the pain and suffering of this earth until He comes to take us home. I began to shake and sob uncontrollably. I knew it was the Holy Spirit crying inside of me at the wall of oppression this group was under that didn't allow them to see or take in the truth that they had just been taught. Sobbing, knowing that they would leave the building that night and not be changed. They would stay the same and continue to come back week after week without the light of Jesus coming from John's teachings penetrating their lives and changing them forever.

I asked the Holy Spirit if I was to speak up about what I knew was going on, encouraging the group to speak in faith and let go of their fears, but I was not to. He knew it wouldn't be received. I left that night undone at the thought of such a mass of people so filled with hurt and fear and anxiety, who had access to the King of Glory but didn't know how to get to Him. As I stumbled to my prayer closet to discuss the night's events with my Lord, He immediately took me into a vision that clearly explained the plight of many Christians in our day.

The Vision

It was Christmas Eve, and the large family of young adult siblings were seated around the living room. There were several brothers and sisters laughing and talking, reminiscing about times gone by. Each also talked of their woes: financial crises they were going through, sicknesses, family troubles. I was seated behind them on the ceiling and had a bird's-eye view of the event. To the right, I watched the mother walk in. She glowed in her Christmas outfit, excitement of a secret surprise bursting on her face. She pulled behind her a cart that was overflowing with presents, each a large box wrapped exquisitely in the finest paper with a large bow atop, bearing the name of the recipient on it. She didn't speak a word, just smiled as she handed out present after present. When the last adult child had received a gift, she said that she had one more present for them all to share. Out from behind her stepped the dad. His face wore the lines of hard work and exhaustion. But his smile was one to light the room. The excitement he exuded about the gifts his children were about to open poured from his every fibre.

He said, "I know that I have been gone for a while, but I was traveling abroad and working very hard to be able to purchase the gifts that I have given you. It was with a great deal of suffering, hurt, and hard work that I was able to obtain the gifts, and what you are about to unwrap will change your lives forever. Each smaller gift inside the box comes with instructions—if you use it the way I have told you, your life on this earth will forever be blessed. Go ahead, open your gifts." I turned from listening to the dad to watch the children rip open their boxes with excitement. Inside the boxes were several smaller items. A ticket that resembled a lottery ticket with instructions stating it was the bank passbook to their trust fund he had put in place for them. The trust fund held enough money to take care of every need and desire they would ever have on earth. Another card resembling a government-issue health card, the instructions stating that while the children carried the cards, sickness would never come upon them again, and that they could loan out the cards to others who were ill and the healing properties in the cards would make them well also. There were several small boxes and cards in the large box, each holding keys of not only promised but already set aside provisions and bounty for the rest of their lives. I glanced back at the dad. He was absolutely beaming! He was so excited to give these gifts to his children, to see all his years of hard work come to fruition as presents in their hands. But then suddenly, the smile faded away. His faced turned long, and tears welled up in his eyes. As I looked back at his family, I saw that none of them were jumping up and down with excitement; no one even came over to hug him or say thank you. In horror, I watched with the parents as each child turned the presents over in their hands, stared at them for a while, and said things like, "That's nice. Thanks, Dad. Isn't he great?" with mindless monotone words. Each put the gifts back in the big outer box, pulled the torn paper over the top and replaced the bow in a shoddy mess, and then stuffed the boxes under their chairs. These siblings then went on about their conversations as before, discussing their hurts and sicknesses and fears, as if nothing had happened! I couldn't believe what I was seeing! How could they? How could they hurt their dad so much? He obviously had been gone a very long time working hard to make sure that they would be taken care of their entire lives, in every area, and no one could even go over to him to say thank you! I was in shock. I looked back at the parents. Mom hugged the dad with encouragement and kissed him tenderly, shrugging her shoulders. With tears in his eyes, he left. No one noticed. No one cared that he had come, and no one noticed that he had left. The incredible gifts he had borne remained under their chairs. As I watched from my vantage point on the ceiling, the family members got up one by one as the evening wore on, leaving the party, and leaving their gifts behind. The gifts gathered dust. The mom quietly, with a torn sadness sweeping across her face, gathered each tattered package from beneath the chairs and put them back on the cart, never to be opened again.

Sobbing intensely, I cried out to my God, begging for forgiveness for times when I had put His gift under my chair and chosen to ignore Him instead. When I chose my pity partying and accepting whatever the devil has thrown at me instead of appropriating the gifts from heaven that He had provided for me. *Forgive me, Lord!* I didn't need an explanation of the vision, but He chose to give me one anyway.

The siblings represent the majority of the Christian church body. It is significant that they are young adults in the vision. This shows that they are not "baby Christians." These are people who may have grown up in the church or have been there long enough to have heard and been part of foundational teachings. They have an understanding of who God the Father is, who Jesus is and what He did for us, and who the Holy Spirit is. People who should know what the Word says regarding the woes they are going through. The mom represents the church leadership, the conduit through which Father comes corporately. Yes, each child of God can go directly to Him via our Great High Priest Jesus, but for the vision's sake, Mom is church leadership that carries the responsibility of teaching and guiding the church body corporately. The dad? Obvious. Father God. The present's symbolism is twofold. First, the wrapper: exquisite paper and gorgeous bow trim—Jesus Himself. Coming to us in all His glory. Not a baby in a manger. Not a beaten body hanging defeated on a cross. But a King enrobed in kingly garments, the finest of anything ever crafted. A present to humans more glorious than anything we could ever conjure in our wildest imaginations. Jesus. The gifts inside are symbolic of everything Jesus's sacrifice accomplished, not only for our eternal life beyond earth's gates, but for what He has set aside for us right now for this life on earth.

Smaller tidbits from this vision. Dad's behavior. The dad did not barge into the room, he did not demand their respect or acknowledgement, and he did not press them for acclamations for the gifts he gave them. He waited. And when no response was offered, he exited. They knew he wouldn't ever abandon them; his gift was proof of that. Even when he wasn't around, he was still looking out for them and had their best interests always on his mind and in his tasks. But he didn't expect them to love him in return. This dad's behavior is synonymous with our free will. Father God does not push us to love Him. He offers His love and His gift of Jesus freely, and we are free to take it or free to pass it by. He will never leave us or forsake, but should we choose to ignore Him, He will not press us, despite the pain and hurt it causes Him.

The siblings' behavior is synonymous with the majority of professed Christians out there. More than willing to go to church. More than willing to take the gifts that "Mom"—leadership—hands to them. But then not willing to hear Father God speak to them beyond Mom. Not willing to read the instructions for themselves and follow through. Unable to translate the teaching into faith that moves the mountains in their lives, as they are unwilling—or unable due to numerous reasons—to hear the Holy Spirit as He guides them in the instructions on how to change their lives and live in the bounty Father has provided for them. Content to sit in the building, chat with others about the woes they have, take the gift for the moment, and then go home, symbolically leaving it under the chair. Instantly squashing the revelation or truth that was offered by the leadership by speaking out about their physical trials. Not *appropriating* (there's that word again) the reality of the blessings heaven holds for them, which they can receive just by asking for them!

As I write this I am reminded that I too fall into the "they" category every now and then. I forget the blessings I have and the ones that are waiting for me. I succumb to sickness because I left my "covenant health card" at home on the dresser and either choose to neglect my body and let a sickness enter or choose to sin and open the door to sickness and pain that way—yes, I said sickness is my fault. But that's another story. I whine about my lack of money and then remember that the "covenant passbook" states that my trust fund is full; I just have to follow the instructions and tithe to access it.

Mom's behavior. Gentle, excited, comforting. Mom is so excited about Dad's gifts that she gets to give her children. She took incredible time to place each item in the box. Wrapped each one with precise diligence to ensure its pristine beauty reaches the beholder. She carefully hands it to each one, gingerly passing it on due to the extreme value of what is inside. When the party is over, her disappointment shrouds her face as she retrieves the left-behind packages of love unwanted. Tucks them away in her cart, hopeful that the next time her family comes together, someone will take the present home with him or her. How often is this the plight of a pastor? Hours spent in prayer and dissecting of the Word, imagination exploding to prepare a presentation for the church each Sunday that will instantly be pleasing and attention-getting to their spiritual eyes and ears. Packaging the love and Father's gifts in their sermons so that when the hearers hear, they will instantly receive it with joy and thank Dad above for the amazing gift coming from the one speaking. Finishing with a moving conclusion that will spur the congregation on to growth, further intimacy with their Lord, and physical movement to advance the kingdom of heaven on earth. But as hands are shaken while parishioners exit, the pastor listens to the low murmurs of pain and darkness seeping from each one's words. Another Sunday where the gifts were left under the seats. Another Sunday where most of the congregation will go home, eat their lunch, and continue on with life as normal, completely forgetting what they have just been given and not understanding how the gift could change their lives.

I wasn't to share the vision with the group the next week, or ever. Instead, it was something between me and Dad, to help me always remember compassion. Always remember that I cannot possibly know why other people behave the way they do or why they just don't "get it" when the teaching comes to light in them. I was never to judge or speak out harshly when fellow believers didn't react the same way that I did. But also to give me an understanding in how to pray when I witnessed the scenario again. How to pray outwardly in love with the group to break down the hidden walls and incite them to believe, and how to pray inwardly with the Holy Spirit's guidance to come against the forces of darkness that loomed over the person. I was to remember that although I was in an incredible upswing of faith in my life at that time, many times I am not. And when those times come, I too put the box under the chair. I too walk out of the party talking about my woes instead of bringing home the cure that was given to me.

If we could all remember the inner—"for right now"—gifts tucked away inside the outward wrapping of Jesus, we truly would live out our lives "on earth, as it is in heaven." My children pray and expect to see something happen. They know that their God hears their prayers and that something will happen in the natural world as their words are carried in the supernatural. They get it. Jesus told us, "Assuredly, I say to you, whoever does not receive the kingdom of God as a little child will by no means enter it" (Mark 10:15). Childlike faith. Easy. Black and white. Simple. If we can believe as a child does, we will enter the kingdom, right now, here on earth.

Chapter 3

Working It Out

> Therefore, my beloved, as you have always
> obeyed, not as in my presence only, but now
> much more in my absence, work out your own
> salvation with fear and trembling, for it is God
> who works in you both to will and to do for His
> good pleasure.
>
> —Philippians 2:12–13

I had just walked away from a long, bad relationship. Thinking we should try again, we got back together. Seven days in, on my birthday, he pushed me off the steps down onto the ground and told me he never, ever wanted to see me again, along with some other choice words. I was finished.

We had been together for a few years, and our relationship, to say the least, was less than pleasant. With both of us coming out of hurtful pasts, the union was doomed from the start. As I stumbled down the driveway to my car, I felt like everything in me had died. All that was left was my body. Not remembering the drive back to my apartment, I stumbled in the door and crawled to the kitchen. Without thinking or rationalizing, as there was no more room for rationalizing, I contemplated which knife would do the job the quickest. Choosing my large butcher knife, I made the long walk down the hall to my bedroom. Zombie. Not seeing. Not hearing. No thoughts. Just a lifeless body floating toward eternal damnation.

As I lay on my bed, final thoughts passed through my head. What about my mom? How would she take the news? She was the only one I was really concerned about. I didn't feel like anyone else would notice that I was gone. I didn't matter to anyone, and everything I had was now shattered. The devil whispered that she would be glad I was gone and wouldn't have to put up with the burden of me any longer. I agreed. As I put the knife to my throat, I heard something in my kitchen. Like it mattered. But still, I jumped to my feet to go and see. As expected, there was nothing there. Shaken, I stumbled back to my bed to finish what needed to be done. The spirit of Suicide was mad now. He realized what was going on, and he wasn't going to allow his plans to go unfulfilled. He turned up the heat and turned up his voice: *"Do it! Do it! Do it! Everyone hates you You are worthless. You are useless. Do it!"* he shouted in my head. Once again, I put the knife to my throat to end it all.

Then a larger-than-life voice called my name: *"Alison!"*

I thought, *What was that?* I knew I had heard it. I had heard it with my own ears. Like someone standing right beside my bed screaming my name at me. After lying there a few moments longer, completely convinced I had now lost my mind, I again picked up the knife.

But then, again I heard it. My name bellowing out from an unseen mouth: *"Alison!"*

My thoughts raced back to schoolgirl teachings of Samuel and the Lord calling out his name. I asked, as Samuel had, "Is that you, Lord?" to which He replied, *"Daughter, I love you."* That's it. Nothing more. *"Daughter, I love you."* He knew what it would take to save my life. He knew that I just needed one person, other than my mom, to tell me that he or she loved me and that I was worth staying on this planet for. He knew what my life had in store for me. He just needed me to stay here so I could fulfill it. I laid down that knife, promising to never pick it up again, if He would just love me. More tears fell that night than have ever fallen again. The Holy Spirit met me there in my room and comforted and loved me with the Father's love. I didn't leave my room for several days afterward. I couldn't.

It was almost three years and many sins later that I met my Jesus in person and gave my life to Him. But the entire time, He never left me. All I had known prior was false religion that taught works equal salvation. But at that moment in time, He taught me that works were for naught. That calling on His name is all that is required. Believing He can and will save us if we would just ask Him to.

I was destined for eternal damnation that birthday. The devil had a plan. It almost came to fruition. But even when I had turned away from the God I had been taught about and the religion that had enslaved me, the real Jesus never left. His eyes were not closed to my pain. He still counted every tear and was waiting for the moment in time when I would respond to His beckoning. He knew my end from my beginning. He knew. And He called. Thank you, Jesus, for calling.

That night, I heard His voice. Although three years passed before I gave my life to Him, I never forgot it. But someone else also did not forget that night. The enemy will always be ready to take advantage of spiritual open doors that we swing wide by purposeful sin. Suicide thoughts or actions are not exempt. It doesn't matter whether you are saved or unsaved. The devil hung around the cracked-open door of suicidal tendencies from teenagerhood, saw the wide-open door into my life that night—and took it.

Suicide Hanging Around

Six feet tall and one hundred pounds by age twelve. If you are a model, fabulous. If you are an insecure child trapped in an adult-sized body, horrific. I grew incredibly fast, suffered through years of growth pains in my legs as they seemingly stretched inches at a time in a one-night span, and came upon puberty with no introduction or welcome wagon. I was kept sheltered from boys and dating and media, told all of that was wrong and horrible and dangerous. By grade seven, I was lanky and unstable from my height, with feet that never quite caught up to a size that could easily support my stature. My lack of weight included lack of breasts, which made it open season in the jokes and teasing department. As my fellow classmates grew eyelashes and makeup and fashionable clothing, I grew pimples and pants that were always too short. The lack of breasts caused me to slouch, hunching my shoulders, so no one would notice. The lack of self-esteem made the slouch easy, and the constant onslaught of verbal arrows from others telling me to stop slouching and straighten up made me do it even more. I was always in the last two to be picked for sports or teams of any kind—me and the really geeky kid. I always inwardly begged for me to not be the last one. Most of the time, I was.

At the end of grade eight, we moved to a new city, where I knew no one. I began high school completely on my own, knowing only one person, our papergirl. Grade nine gym class seemed to last forever, with never-ending teasing by classmates on my looks, my clothes, my badly permed hair, my pimple-covered face, and my incredible lack of coordination in any sports event. I was beaten to a pulp in dodgeball and scared to death to show up on the field hockey turf, as I knew it would mean weeks of bruised shins and hamstrings from the inevitable stick slashes from the popular girls. Changing in the locker room petrified me.

By the end of grade nine, I had made one other friend. She too was an outcast because of bad choices made, and she suffered terrible teasing and verbal abuse as well. Together, we consoled each other and became strongholds for each other in school. However, being raised as a Jehovah's Witness, I was not allowed to be on any school teams, join the band, or even associate with schoolmates outside of school. It was drilled into me that anyone who was not a Witness was a "bad association who spoiled useful habits," and I was only to choose to be around other Witness children. As we had moved to the new city, the only Witness children that I knew were the ones in my new congregation, who lived on the other side of the city and went to the other high school. I was the only one at my school. So I had my friend at school, but at home, unless my mom would drive me across the city, I had no one.

My brothers are ten and five years older than me, and by the time I entered high school, they were finished and were off driving and living their own lives. I felt so alone. Alone became a friend for me. I remember sitting for hours on the front lawn, just hoping someone from school would drive by and see me and stop to say hi. They didn't. I would walk the high school corridors with my head hanging down, my shoulders hunching so much that they looked as if they might touch in front. By the end of grade ten, I had learned to chameleon into groups so I could at least be included. I learned that if I did the popular boys' homework and was their partner in class, they would say hi to me. I learned that if I laughed at people's jokes that I didn't think were funny, they would include me. I learned that if I worked incredibly hard and got excellent grades, the teachers would applaud me. I also learned that if I smiled all the time and jumped around as if happy and excited, people wouldn't know how sad I was inside. I was the clown on the outside, but dying on the inside. A beautiful fourteen-year-old girl with an awesome life and wonderful parents who loved her, but all she could see was loneliness.

I hadn't ever heard the word *suicide* until the end of grade ten. I didn't know what it was. Then one of my classmates taught me. We weren't friends, and I didn't even know her, but I do remember the announcement over the PA system. I remember her empty chair. And to me, it sounded like a good idea. I began to think about it. How I would do it. Where. What I would use. How it would end the teasing. End the pain of loneliness I felt every single day. But then I would think about how it would devastate my mom, and she is what kept me from doing it. I couldn't do it to her. I knew that would kill her, and I couldn't be responsible for her death. I talked about it with my school friend. She had thought about it too. Her teasing was even more vicious than mine. I mentioned it to my Witness friend. She too had thought about and contemplated it.

What we didn't know was that as we spoke of it and discussed it and contemplated it, we opened the door for the spirit of Suicide to come into our lives and begin to set down roots. One of the most aggressive of evil spirits there is, Suicide heard his invitation to our open door of sadness and took full advantage of it. TV shows suddenly always had a suicide in the story. I heard of it more and more on the radio, read about it in magazines, saw highlights of it on the evening news. Was it that it was more rampant than it had been earlier in my life? No. It was that I was now aware of it, and Suicide was on my shoulder, bringing it to my attention at every opportunity. Whispering in my ear what an easy way out it would be. Reminding me that I could end all the pain and mental agony with one easy slice.

And then someone else I knew did it. And we were all dumbfounded, frightened, stunned, and numb. All of us said, "How could she? She had a great life, great parents, a car, did well in school, was popular," but we all knew the torture that she endured because she was overweight and was teased about it. Although most of us Witness kids talked secretly about suicide, she talked openly about it. The spirit of Suicide had almost full control of that girl in the last year of her life, and then complete control on her last day. Suicide murdered her that summer night. She came to a party, seemingly happy, and then began to talk about committing suicide. As she had talked a lot about it, we didn't pay too much attention, just brushed her off. We really thought she was just like us—just thought about it but wasn't serious. But that night, she was. Suicide whispered long enough until eventually, she listened.

By the time I graduated high school, Suicide was becoming one of my best friends whom I spoke with daily. He was there when I awoke in the morning, reminding me that I could end it all and not ever have to battle a tortuous day of teasing again and there at night to show me pictures in my mind of me slicing my throat, putting one of Dad's handguns to my temple, or taking a walk out to the woods with a shotgun. Upon entering my twenties, I went to my doctor and asked for antidepressants. I was told that depression was hereditary, and as both my parents and brothers were on antidepressants, he was surprised that I had waited so long for them. Antidepressants made it possible for me to get up in the morning and go to work, but each day started with a friendly reminder from my shoulder buddy Suicide that no drugs would make him go away, and if I just ended it all, everything would be better. I would put myself and everyone around me out of our miseries if I just exited. I spent ages twenty to twenty-six making terrible choices that added to my self-hatred, and on my twenty-seventh birthday, I finally yielded to Suicide's beckonings. As I lay on my bed with a knife at my throat, I cried and thought, *This is it. There is finally no one left who cares about me, and no one will miss me. I will be doing everyone a favor. This is the best thing.*

But the God whom I had learned about in my years of religious training still cared. Although I had left the religion years earlier due to its hypocrisy and false teachings that I had uncovered and had made an oath to myself to *never* fall victim to religious abuse again, the true Father in heaven never *left* me. The god I had learned about was not the real One. The one I had learned about was a tyrannical communist who demanded unwavering subordination from all his subjects, or else he rejected them and applauded his other subjects who rejected the insubordinate as well. *That* was not the real God in heaven. My real Father in heaven knew my hurt, my pain, and my anguish. He saw the atrocities that were done to me. He felt the pain that I felt. And at my last, weakest moment, the moment when He knew I would hear Him and listen, He called.

The next few days after hearing His voice, I was in a daze. I wandered around and was completely unaware of anything happening around me. And then Suicide paid me a visit. And he determined that if he couldn't get me to actually kill myself outright, he would convince me to self-destruct with abusive behavior. The Voice I had heard and fallen in love with in that one moment in time seemed to fade into the recesses of my mind with the onslaught of life-numbing choices I now had in front of me.

Three years went by before I acted on the love invitation from the Voice I had heard so long before. I met my Jesus and heard His voice once again, as I had heard years before. He healed me of depression and all the other chronic physical ailments that had tortured my body for most of my life. But Suicide still hung out at night. Although I was no longer depressed and truly loved life and my Jesus, there he was at night. Hanging out on my pillow. Ready and poised and waiting for me to close my eyes. Once my eyes were closed, he would immediately send images of me killing myself into my mind's eye. I would see the knife at my throat, the gun at my temple. Although I had repented of the years of suicidal talk, thoughts, and attempts, the images were still there in my mind's eye, tormenting me each night.

As I felt incredible guilt over these thoughts and images that were ever-present, and did not understand that the demon of suicide was throwing them in there, I told no one. Then one night at a friend's house during a worship service, when my big toe spiritual curse was uncovered (that's another story later on), Suicide decided he would hide out. But my intuitive friends heard the Holy Spirit's voice, and He advised them that there was another demon lurking beneath the surface of my skin, hiding. My friends asked me who it was. I heard the demon speak from inside my head, into my mind, "Don't tell them. Don't tell them, or I will kill you."

I cried out, "Suicide! It's the spirit of suicide!" at which my friend commanded it to leave my body and never torture me again. *Working out my salvation with fear and trembling.* My spirit was saved. Now it was my body's turn. My body convulsed, I felt the demon exit up my throat and out my mouth, and that was it. After much wonderful ministering by friends to me, I went home and went to bed. And as I fell into the world of restful sleep, I suddenly awoke and realized that it was the first time in *years* that I had closed my eyes and not seen myself with a knife at my throat! Praise God! The demon was gone, and so was the torture in my mind! How long I had lived with this mental agony each and every night. I thought I had to. I thought that because I had had these thoughts for so long, and had entertained them willingly for so long, they would be with me for the rest of my life. But that is not what my Jesus tells me. That is not what the Word tells me. He tells me that His sacrifice is enough. His blood is enough to wash away all my sins and the entire residue that they left behind. I just had to appropriate it. I had to walk under the waterfall of it and ask for it.

Lesson learned? When we open the door to sin, sin comes in. And as long as we continue to *willingly* operate in that sin, the demon that goes along with it will lurk around, oppress us, influence us, come into our bodies, and continue to encourage us to sin (Genesis 4:7). But once that sin is repented of, there is no longer any legal ground for that demon to stay in our bodies or our presence. However, if we do not tell that demon to leave, it may hang around unnoticed. It may continue to influence us without our being aware of it. That is what happened to me. I confessed and repented of my sin of suicidal thinking, but the demon behind the influence was never told to leave. So he continued to torture my mind. We must, as children of the living God, be aware of the spirit realm, acknowledge the reality of demons and angels, understand our authority in Christ, and *exercise* it!

Demons at My Window

Ryan and I loved to watch movies. Romantic comedies are my favorite. Ryan prefers action thrillers. Before meeting Jesus, we had hundreds of movies that we watched regularly. However, within months of giving our lives to Jesus, we both became very convicted about the movies we were watching and began to purge our collection. Obvious "bad" movies went in the trash. Horrors, extreme violence, sexual flicks—all thrown out. But there were a few that we really, really laughed at, and although not extreme in what some might consider extreme badness, they weren't by any means God honoring. We couldn't bring ourselves to get rid of those. Those had wormed their way into our hearts, and although it shouldn't have, it took a bit more encouragement from the Holy Spirit for us to trash them.

A few more months passed, and we continued to study, learn, and grow in our relationship with Jesus. Then one evening, we were sitting watching a movie, and suddenly I was taken into a vision. It was as if I had been removed from my body and was sitting up at the ceiling in the corner. I could see myself and Ryan sitting on the couch eating our popcorn and watching the movie. Out of the corner of my eye, I saw movement outside our living room window. Turning my head in my vision, I saw demonic faces plastered against the window watching the movie with us. Looking back at the TV, in my vision we were watching a romantic comedy where two unmarried men crash weddings to try to pick up the bridesmaids. They woo them, have sex with them, and leave in the morning. Gross fornication and coarse language all wrapped up in a big comedy bow. Make the dialogue funny and the sin being glorified doesn't seem so bad anymore. As I looked at the movie, I heard a demon's voice. Turning back to the window, I saw the demon call out over his shoulder, "Hey, Fornication, they're watching a movie that glorifies you. You're in, buddy!" Instantly, the spirit of Fornication morphed through our living room window, sat down on our couch between us, and began eating my popcorn! I was in shock.

In the vision, Ryan flipped the channel to another movie, this time an action thriller. It too was one that we had not thrown away in our first round of purging. Drug trafficking, prostitution, police turned bad. This one wrapped up in a good-looking actor's bow that made the swearing palatable. I looked back to the window. The demon leader again yelled out over his shoulder, "Hey, Violence, they're watching one of your shows! You're in too!" In morphed the spirit of Violence, along with his friends Murder and Deception. They too squeezed in on my couch, put their arms around our shoulders, and enjoyed the show.

The final round was when Ryan flipped the channel to a horror movie. Although we had gotten the conviction on these movies months earlier and had thrown out the few we had, my Jesus needed to make sure I understood the point. As the horror movie played on in the vision, I turned my head to see the worst thing of all. The demon leader turned and yelled, "Hey, Boss, they're having a party in your name!" at which point Satan himself came into my house, along with every other demon that was hanging around outside.

This vision took literally thirty seconds to play through, from the time the Lord took me into it in my mind's eye to the time it was over, but I will be forever changed by it. In real time, immediately the movie was all done for me. I got up from the couch sobbing and went to my room. I was all done. All done by God's grace, that He allows us to continue in ignorance when He has every right to destroy us for our blatant dishonoring of who He is. All done by my stupidity in thinking that what I allow into my home through the TV or radio doesn't have any effect on the spiritual atmosphere around me. All done by His love, that He would show me the reality of every choice that I make.

From that time forward, I have hardly been able to watch anything that comes out of Hollywood. Murder mysteries, prime-time TV police shows, and sitcoms no longer come into our home. Our gracious Lord showed us the reality of the spiritual atmosphere around us. Showed us that every choice we make either opens or closes a door for the angelic or the demonic to come into our homes and influence us. In my years of ministering to fellow believers, the Holy Spirit makes me aware within moments of listening to the person that a great deal of many people's problems come from what they allow into their homes via movies, music, and books.

The devil has done a fantastic job of training Hollywood to make us believe it is just "a movie." Just entertainment. "It's not a big deal, Alison. You are making a big deal out of nothing. We watch it for the graphics; they are so cool. It's really not influencing me. I just think watching blood and gore is funny." These are some of the many, many comments I have heard when I am prompted to share the vision I was given. Disappointingly, many of these comments have come from church leaders that we have known. The reality of it is that there is a second heaven out there that is filled with demons. Those demons are intent on murdering each and every one us, and if you belong to Jesus, you have a big giant bull's-eye on your forehead. We must get an understanding of this reality and cease to live as if it is not there. Many people have accused me of being a fanatic who thinks there is a demon lurking behind every bush to get me. They're wrong. I think there are two demons behind every bush! We as followers of Jesus must be aware of the murderous plot against us! Does my awareness make me fearful? Am I looking behind every bush and sidestepping as I walk by? No. I am confident in the promises written in His Word stating that my foot will not stumble and that although ten thousand may fall at my right hand, no danger will come near me. But that does not mean that I can go and blatantly invite the devil into my home and not expect the ramifications of darkness to follow.

With the next movie that you watch, take a look out your window.

Initiation into Deliverance and Physical Manifestations

What you are about to read happened twelve years ago from the time of writing it today. When it was all done and the week of torture was over, my dear friend and pastor told me to write it down. She said that someday God would ask me to retell this story and that I would appreciate that I had written it down. He would use the story to help others. I, of course, did not write it down. I didn't at the time think that anyone would ever want to hear what I had to say, so why bother? As well, it was one of the most frightening weeks of my life, scared me to the deepest core, and was not something that I would ever want to retell. In the past twelve years I don't think I have repeated this story more than maybe three times, and even now my heart is racing as I rethink the details of the trial. It was the closest I have ever come to touching the darkness of the devil, and I never want to go there again. However, in my current obedience, my Lord is asking me to recount the details of that week for you, the reader, so that from what I went through, others may be comforted. As you read, what I say may not align with what you have been taught regarding demons and their allowed access to Christians. However, I ask that you read with an open mind, just reading it as *my* story, and then ask the Holy Spirit to direct you in what you are to take from it. What I know is the physical reality of what happened in and around my body for that week-long ordeal, and that cemented in my spirit the reality of the supernatural world around me.

It had been two years since meeting Jesus and asking Him to be my Lord and Savior. Our church had begun a weekly women's prayer meeting, and I had joined in. I love to pray corporately and knew I was to be a part of this group. As the church was large and full of different ministries throughout the week, there wasn't one night that we could have the entire building to ourselves. So we met on the same night as another ministry, us in the library and them in the main hall. Following a time of praise, we would move into intercession for our country and government, then for the local churches, and then for individual prayer cards from our church family. This particular evening, there were only three of us there to pray. As we moved from praying for the church body to praying for individuals, my teeth began to chatter. I wasn't cold, but I couldn't stop the chattering. One of the other ladies didn't notice, but one did. Her antennae were up, and she was instantly alerted to the movement of the enemy within my body.

When I prayed out loud, it would stop as long as I was talking. But as soon as I stopped talking, the chattering would begin. As we ended our time of prayer and the first lady left, the second one stopped me from leaving and instructed me to go upstairs, find the pastor's wife, and tell her about my teeth. Still very new in my faith and not ever hearing anything about demonic possession or that it was even possible for saved Christians to be possessed by demons, I didn't understand why. She explained that she had to get home to her children and what was going to happen might take a while, but I was to go immediately, get the pastor's wife, and tell her what was going on; then she would know what to do. Okay, obedient little one that I was, I marched upstairs and sought out my pastor's incredible wife, Wanda. As the other ministry was due to finish up within a half hour, she took me aside to her office and calmly explained that in our lives prior to Jesus, we allow demons to come into our bodies through our life choices. Then, after meeting Jesus, sometimes some of them will hide, and we have to work them out. Some people are never free of all the demons that oppress them, and that is why they continue to make bad choices throughout their lives. Others, however, when they press into God and continuously seek Him and seek reconciliation, repentance and spiritual growth, force these demons to come to the surface because they cannot stand being in our bodies any longer due to our worship of God. She advised me that she was going to pray over me and tell the demons to leave me. But what happened next neither of us was prepared for. Although I am writing this years later, it is still as clear as yesterday.

Wanda prayed a prayer of thanks and praise and then in

Jesus's name told the demon to leave. What happened next inside my body was horrid and the most bizarre acknowledgement of the true and real separation of soul and body that we have. I felt the actual, tangible presence of the demon inside of me. I felt it come up from my gut, through my throat and into my face, literally pushing my soul out to the side of my face as it used my eyes to look out. I felt it using my eyeballs to see out of my body and stare at Wanda. I felt the hellish hatred it had for her as it looked out of my body at her. It then took over my mouth and seethed out in the most disgusting, perverted, straight-from-a-horror-movie voice, "I hate youuuuu. You disgust meeeee." I was mortified! *What if Wanda thinks this is me saying this? I love her as a sister! She was one of my best friends! How can I be saying this to her?* But I wasn't. It was the "it" stealing my body that was saying it. My mouth then began to spit at her. My hands reached out to grab her, and I knew the demon intended to harm her physically. I screamed and told it to stop in Jesus's name! The Holy Spirit took over Wanda, and she began to militantly command the demons to leave. She called them out by name as the Holy Spirit led her. As she called out each demon by name, it screamed through my voice as it left my body and gave a very physical manifestation of its departure. On the outside, she physically held my wrists so I couldn't punch her. My mouth spat on her, my feet kicked out at her, and my head twisted so far left and right that I thought it was going to rip off. I convulsed and threw up green venom on our feet. With all of this going on outside of my body, my soul sat helpless in the corner on the inside of my body, incapable of participating in the battle. I watched it happening, the demons taking over my body and attacking one of my best friends, and I had no control over anything my body was doing.

At least an hour had now gone by, and the leader of the other ministry knocked on the door to ask if everything was okay. She, and many others from the group, had heard me screaming and knew her help was required. Wanda firmly instructed her to come inside and pray out loud over me as she continued the battle. Another half hour went by, and Wanda asked the Lord for protection and angelic forces to be with me for the rest of the evening. She was spent and could do no more. I was limp and physically incapable of moving. But I knew there was more lurking in the deep lower recesses of my body. I could feel them. I could hear them in my ears. I literally felt hell in my body. It was disgusting. Dirt and hatred, venom and perversion spiralling around inside of me. As I tried to walk, I was ridiculously dizzy and nauseated. I told Wanda I was incapable of driving. The other leader had to drive my vehicle home for me, and her husband followed behind in their van. Once home, I couldn't walk. They got Ryan, and he carried me from the van to the front door. Briefly explaining what had happened to me, she quickly departed. Ryan, unaware of the seriousness of the matter, got me into the house and left me in the front hall. As I stepped into the living room, round two for the evening began.

I felt like a burning fireball had been flung at me and struck me in the chest, and down I went. My body went into demonic convulsions, and I screamed for Ryan to come and get me. I couldn't stand up. He helped me to my feet, and as soon as he let go, it happened again. I dropped to the floor screaming as the demons welled up to the surface in my body. Trying to explain to my bewildered husband what was happening, I was overcome with the reality of demons in our house. We had recently been given a piece of furniture by a personal friend who was involved in Wicca, and instantly I knew there were demons attached to it. Suddenly full of renewed energy fuelled by hatred for the very things that were oppressing me, I ran to the bedroom, grabbed the footboard, and screamed to every demon attached to it to leave the bed and leave my house immediately! The bed began to bounce on the floor, and then *boom!* A huge fireball wind blasted out of it, hit Ryan, who was standing in the doorway, and knocked him to the side; then it whirled around the hall into my kitchen. I ran to the kitchen door, opened it, and screamed that the demon was to leave my house and never return! I am quite sure that my elderly neighbor was now very worried about her new neighbors, who had just moved in a short while ago (that would be me!).

I sat on the kitchen floor and cried, trying to explain to Ryan what was going on. He helped me up to bed, and I begged my God to let sleep come and for this to be over. Sleep did come, but it was far from over. The following morning, I was to meet my neighborhood prayer team. As my feet hit the floor I was instantly jolted back into the reality of the evening before. My head reeled at the events of the night and the instant learned lesson of the reality of demons. I felt nausea. My legs were weak. I prayed and asked my God to get me to the end of the street. *Just get me to my neighbor's house and she can pray for me. Let me keep it together and not scare my fifteen-month-child with physical manifestations.* Interestingly enough, the entire ordeal with the bed happened right across the hall from where my daughter was sleeping—me screaming, the bed bouncing—and she slept right through it.

Flu-like symptoms haunted me as I bundled Genevieve into her snowsuit and staggered down the street. When my neighbor came to the door, I asked her to get her children to take care of Genevieve and for her to take me downstairs and pray with me immediately. The urgency in my voice and the strain in my face told her what she was in for. As soon as Genevieve was secure with the other children, the physical manifestations kicked in again. I couldn't walk and couldn't speak; I felt my soul pushed out of the way. She prayed in the authority of Jesus's name over me, admonishing the demons that they were not allowed to harm me or Genevieve. She instructed me to call my pastors and have them come and pray with me immediately, as she had to get her children off to school. Home again, phone calls made, Genevieve to the sitter, me to the church.

When I stumbled back to Wanda's office, she and Pastor Bruce realized the intensity of my need for deliverance from the demons torturing me. Bruce, normally calm and mild in his tone of voice, began to pray in militant fashion, telling me to focus and asking me what I was hearing inside my head and what I was feeling was going on in my body. Although the details of this time of prayer are now unclear, I remember that a good deal of what transpired before the demons were told to leave was me having to repent for things that I had done that opened the door for the demons to come into my body in the first place.

Unforgiveness, bitterness, and resentment for past events in my life. Hatred and guilt toward myself. Repentance of deliberate sins. As Holy Spirit led Bruce in what to say and he instructed me in what to repent of, he then would speak specifically to that demon who had come in and told it to leave, as the entrance way and legal right it had to stay in my body were now gone due to my repentance. At one point, my foot and leg started jumping up and down as I watched what looked like a snake come up the side of my shin under my skin before it exited in flatulence. At another time, I suddenly had incredible compression pain in my brain, as if an octopus had grasp hold of my head and was squeezing my brain with its tentacles. That afternoon of deliverance exhausted me. When the clock said that we were done due to prior engagements, I knew I was not completely done yet. I could still feel evil lurking in the depths of my body, trying its best to hide under the veil of sin not yet discovered.

The spirit of fear had now taken a good hold of me. Going through this, looking evil in the eye, and feeling it take over my body was enough to make anyone look over his or her shoulder for a really long time. I prayed out loud constantly. I repeated over and over again that I belonged to Jesus and not to the devil and the demons had no place in me. I played worship music in my home nonstop. Loudly. I knew that the demons hated the sound of Jesus's name and the sound of worship to Him even more. If I could keep that playing, they wouldn't want to hang around. For weeks after this, I couldn't walk past the bedroom door where the bed was without running. I would jump past it and slam the bathroom door when I got there. I could hear the demons laughing at me.

The following weeks to come were spent in my prayer closet

beeseeching the Lord to reveal my sin and the open doors where the enemy had been allowed to come in. Movies, music, entertainment, foul jokes, and foul language—all of these opened doors to the darkness waiting outside.

I had suffered from what was diagnosed as "cluster headaches." I would get sharp, shooting pain in my brain, like someone had stabbed a knife into it and then just as quickly ripped it out. The pain would shoot through my head, spiderweb out over my brain, and then just as fast as it came, it would leave. It was so severe that it would cause me to drop to my knees when it happened, or hit the ditch while I was driving. I would also get terrible bladder infections that would last for several days, if not weeks. They would come without warning and leave just the same. After this week of prayer and deliverance from demons, the headaches became worse and worse. What used to be once or twice a month was becoming daily, and then multiple times per day. I became petrified to go into my bedroom closet. I could sense evil in there and became unable to walk past those doors as well. Each time I went in, I would get a cluster headache. One afternoon, after crying out to God asking why these were getting worse, He turned my head to the closet and instructed me to go in and look on a shelf near the back. There, in a box at the back of the closet, were adult novelties that had long been forgotten about. The very presence of these articles from my past held open the door for the devil to torture me. Instantly, the box was taped up and taken to the trash. I was on my knees repenting and asking my Lord to forgive me for not only participating in that kind of perversion but for being ignorant and leaving the articles in my home as an open door entrance to evil. After praying over myself, my closet and entire home, that was the end of the headaches and the bladder infections. At the time of writing, it has been twelve years without either! Praise God! After I got rid of that box and its contents, the spirit of fear left my home as well. Instantly I was able to walk into the closet and past the bedroom without that sense of evil lurking behind the door.

All those times I have heard people say, "The devil made me do it," I now understand. All the times people do heinous crimes and say that they don't remember doing it, that it was like something took over their bodies, I now understand. Although I would never want to go through that week again, it taught me incredible compassion for others who do things that are most horrid in nature. It taught me how to separate the sin from the person. It taught me the truth and reality of the spiritual realm, the reality of demons, and the reality of the dark repercussions of the daily choices we make in our lives.

The few times I have repeated this story, there are always skeptics. Those Christians who do not want to believe that their sicknesses or illnesses could be because of their own sin that has opened the door to the enemy coming in. But my experiences tell me otherwise. Is all sickness self-induced? Absolutely not. The Scriptures are clear on that (John 9:1–3). But they are also very clear that our actions can cause sickness (Proverbs 26:2b).

So much effort, time, tears, and emotion are wasted on healing prayers that never come to fruition. Faith is shaken and hearts are downcast as prayers hit what seems to be a sounding brass ceiling. Black and white faith told me that if my God says that

Jesus is the Great Physician, then I can be completely healed too. Many have called me radical and "out there." I call it black and white. Black and white faith in the daily doings of life that work out to incredible ends. Working out my salvation with fear and trembling wasn't easy in the beginning, and sometimes it was terrifying and physically painful, but the end result has been worth it. I am still working it out. Now working on the deep inner yuck that no longer has any place to hide. Like a splinter in the pinky finger hurts so bad and you have to work and work to get it out, the journey continues.

Chapter 4

Jimmy

Jimmy was a physically and mentally handicapped man who was brought to our church regularly every Sunday by his intervenor. They would sit in the front corner, and Jimmy would rock back and forth, back and forth. He would smile now and then and groan a happy groan, or attempt to clap his hands, but not much else. Communication with Jimmy seemed pointless, as he wouldn't respond, but I am sure that his spirit man inside was saying hello back.

I was very new in my faith when I first saw Jimmy, and I always wondered why nobody prayed for him. I had heard and read a lot about faith healings and laying-on-of-hands healings and lots of other churches having people healed. Jesus had healed me of my chronic sicknesses and diseases; why didn't anyone pray for Jimmy to be healed? It never occurred to me to ask myself why *I* didn't pray for Jimmy. I excused myself. I told myself that I had only been a Christian for a short time, I didn't know how to do it properly, I would offend any "senior" Christians who might be around me because somehow I would be usurping their authority of their greater "time in the Lord" than mine, and the list went on. I really felt unqualified, and the devil confirmed that. I had no understanding of "freely you have received, now freely give" (Matthew 10:8). I had been taught this verse in the context of money, not in the context of God's power in me.

As church administrator, Sunday mornings were busy for me. One particular morning, after doing my before-church running around and administrating, I was rushed and late getting into the sanctuary. My family was seated in the front row as normal, and when I got to our seats, Jimmy and his intervenor were seated at the end of the row. I smiled at them, shut down the administrator brain, and turned my focus to worshipping my God. Immediately, once my focus had shifted to Jesus, my hands began to shake. This was fairly new to me, but the Holy Spirit had told me that this was a manifestation of my body reacting to the presence of God. They began to shake more and more at my sides, and then my legs began to bounce. I had been learning from my teacher Holy Spirit that during corporate worship time, it wasn't always about singing physically on the outside while standing with my hands raised, but more about following His direction as He took me into the throne room and doing what I saw going on there. My body manifesting was my cue to pay attention. Many times, I saw worshippers in the throne room with hands raised in adoration, but I also saw beings lying prostrate, down on one knee, down on both knees with hands raised, and down on both knees with faces to the floor in respect and honor toward the King. As it was not common in our church at the time, I had a very difficult time with going onto my knees. Ryan and I generally were the only ones on a regular basis who would assume this position, and I at that time was still incredibly self-conscious about what people would think of me. I remember one time overhearing someone say, "They must have sinned really badly to have to get on their knees!" This morning, as my body shook and I saw the throne room worshippers on their knees, the Holy Spirit told me to do the same. With my self-consciousness came rebellion—not *"No, I won't do it"* rebellion, but more of a whiny, "Please don't ask me to do this, you know how it makes me uncomfortable, please let me stand instead" rebellion. I also knew by now that He would gently ask me three times, and if I didn't respond in obedience within those three times, then His presence would lift off of me, my body would stop shaking, and worship would be flat. Just me singing. No engagement from the other Side. I hated that more than I hated the perceived staring of others. I dropped to my knees on His second request, and as I hit the carpet, my friend Nancy was suddenly by my side! She whispered, "The Holy Spirit told me that you were 'going down' and I was to come and join you in intercession." Bless her obedience and His faithfulness to give me confidence that I was hearing His voice and doing what I had heard Him ask! As the music played on, we began to follow the Holy Spirit's leading and praying in tongues. At first, we didn't know what or whom we were praying for, but as the moments passed, we both knew it was for Jimmy. Our bodies rocked as tears streamed down our faces in intercession for our brother beside us. Before we knew it, the music stopped, and I heard Pastor Bruce calling me up on stage to do the announcements. Wiping away my tears and pushing through the notes, I completed the task and retired to my front row seat exhausted. Bruce got back up to preach, and I settled in to rest. But the Holy Spirit was not done with me yet. My job for the morning was not yet completed.

Within seconds of sitting down, I began to rock once more, my telltale sign to pay attention—the Lord had something to say! Okay, I was listening. "I want you to go and get Bruce, interrupt him, and tell him that I am going to heal Jimmy today. I want you to pray for him with Bruce and the congregation praying in agreement."

What? Did I just hear correctly? "You want me to not only *interrupt* him, but I have to pray for Jimmy and have the entire congregation watching me? Are you kidding me?" My head was reeling. Had this been asked of me today, no problem. But as an eighteen-month baby Christian who was incredibly self-conscious and afraid of praying in front of anyone whom I felt superior to me in any way, no way! I began to cry. I absolutely couldn't do this. Flesh took over. I concluded that this wasn't the Lord's voice. I bound the devil from lying in my head. I told the devil to take a hike. He wasn't going to get me to interrupt the pastor. *God* wouldn't possibly ask me to disrupt order in His church and do this kind of thing; it must be the devil.

I heard Him say, "You know my voice."

"Aghh, I do know your voice, I do!" I cried inwardly. "Okay, fine, it's you. But why me? Okay, I need a sign that this is you *for sure.*" Then I tried to make a deal with Him. *Come on, Alison! Do you not yet know who you are dealing with? Seriously!* But I continued. "If this is You and I am hearing correctly, I am going to look back at Jane (*name changed for anonymity*), and if she looks at me and gives me the nod, then I will know that You have told her that You have told me to do this, and then I will do it." Yes, I know. Severe lack of fear of the Lord and severe disobedience. But I was learning, and He was gracious. I turned around and stared at Jane. Jane was our key corporate intercessor, and I knew she heard the Lord's voice. I was positive He would have told her the same thing as me. Besides, why would He tell me something and not her? She had way more authority than I thought I did.

She could not have missed me. No one else did. I caught the eye of pretty much everyone in my line of sight to her, but her eyes didn't shift. She was intent on hearing what Bruce was preaching. "Oh, come on!" I cried to myself. Really? One more time, the Holy Spirit asked me to get up and interrupt the preaching. I knew I had one chance left. I glanced at the clock, and Bruce was already fifteen minutes into his hour-long sermon. Ooo, I really blew it this time. Now begins the beating myself up part. "You are so dumb. If you had gone and done it immediately, then it would have been a whole lot better than going to do it now. He's fifteen minutes in. He's going to lose his train of thought. You will *really* be interrupting now," and so on. Then the guilts: "This may be the last time Jimmy is in church, and if you don't go and get Bruce, he may never get healed, and he may die tomorrow, and it will be all your fault that he didn't see a whole, healthy body this side of heaven."

One more time, gently but firmly, I heard my Lord say, "Go and get Bruce."

I looked over at Jimmy. He was fidgeting horribly, and his intervenor was getting her coat on. Now or never! *Okay, I will do it!* I had to physically *will* my body to get up, and I ran up to the front of the stage. "Excuse me, Bruce," I squeaked out. "I am so sorry for interrupting, but the Lord has asked me to come and get you, and *you* are to pray for Jimmy, and God is going to heal Jimmy today." (Notice I said *"You* are to pray for Jimmy." No, no, that is not what I was told. I was told to get Bruce and *I* was to pray for Jimmy, with Bruce's backing.)

How he even understood me through my sobbing I have no idea. But Bruce, being the incredibly gracious and kind man that he is, agreed instantly. He told the church what I had advised, and he and I walked over to Jimmy. I asked his intervenor if it was okay for us to pray for him; she asked Jimmy and then gave the nod. Bruce handed the microphone to me. I said no. He said, "Yes, the Lord asked you to do it, go ahead."

The spirit of Fear instantly told me, "How dare you think you can pray in the presence of the pastor? *He* is the pastor, not you! *He* is the spiritual authority in this church, not you! How dare you think that you are capable of doing this thing?! God may have asked you to get Bruce, but he did not ask you to pray for Jimmy!" Instantly. There it was. Lying ratscallion! Fear shouting in my head to shut me down. Fear screaming at me in a pious, religious tone, making me think it was right. I have since learned the sound of this voice and no longer succumb to it. But at that time, I was still ignorant. In my insistence to not do it, Bruce conceded and began to pray for Jimmy. The church body fell silent. You could hear a pin drop. Everyone held their breath as each hoped that what had been promised would come to pass. We had never seen an instant physical healing in our group, but we all wanted to. We all had the passion and the desire and the faith for it. But it didn't happen.

Bruce prayed, we all said amen, the intervenor got Jimmy's coat, and they left. Nothing happened. Nothing that we could see tangibly. But God in His almighty wisdom knew this outcome, knew that this was not so much about healing Jimmy's body that day as it was about teaching the church body a good lesson. As I write this now eleven years later, I am still so sad about that day. I don't know why God didn't make Jimmy's body whole that day, He has never told me. I am sure that someday I will know. Just not today.

After Jimmy left, the congregation remained silent. A heavy weight of God's presence fell over the church building. No one moved. No one spoke. All eyes were on Bruce as he made his way back to the stage. I crawled to the back corner of the sanctuary and wept. I begged God to bring Jimmy back, and I would do it! I would pray for him if He would just give me another chance! *Please give me another chance!* I asked desperately. Jimmy didn't come back in that day, or ever again.

For what seemed like an eternity Bruce stood there and said nothing. He too was undone by the presence of God in the place. When he was finally able to speak, he wasn't finishing his sermon; he was encouraging us to keep pressing God, to keep asking for miracles, signs, and wonders, to keep being obedient to the Holy Spirit when He asks us to do something, whether we see the fruit of it or not. Bless Bruce for his love and graciousness on me. Praise be to God for His not killing me right there for my outright disobedience.

I too was undone as I sulked in the back corner. Shame put me there. Anger, frustration, and guilt kept me there. I didn't hear the rest of what Bruce said, and I don't remember what led up to this, but I did hear Bruce ask the congregation that each one who wanted to move more in miracles and each one who wanted more of what had taken place that morning to happen to them as well should raise their hands. Shame had my head in my knees, but gently, there He was. There was my Holy Spirit ever so gently telling me to look up. That was one of the hardest things I had ever done. Lifting my head at that moment was even harder than going up and interrupting Bruce a half hour earlier! But when I did, God in His graciousness opened my physical eyes to see angels flying above the heads of the congregation. And over each one who lifted a hand to ask for more, an angel flew and touched the top of that person's head. As they touched them, I saw what looked like water ripple out after a stone has been dropped in a pond. I watched in amazement and awe as this went on and on. Still no one spoke. No one dared move. All eyes and hearts were focused on Jesus, and as they maintained their focus there, He met their inward cry and adoration with ministering angels. The Holy Spirit invited me to lift my hand as well. I cried inside as the fear and shame told me I wasn't worthy. I didn't deserve more, seeing how I hadn't even used what He had given already me. But this time, I chose to listen the first time when asked to do something by Holy Spirit. I lifted my hand. And for a brief moment longer, Father God allowed my physical eyes to remain open to the spirit realm and allowed me to watch the angel come to me and touch my head. Warm, liquid love flooded my body, which reassured me that life is all a lesson of learning and nothing had been lost today, but much had been gained. His love washed shame from my face and fear off my back that morning. Imagine a mother picking up a crying, shame-filled child who has recklessly broken her favorite china, reassuring the child that it really doesn't matter and that she still adores and will still trust the child; that is what He infused into me with that angel's touch.

As I look back, this lesson had nothing to do with Jimmy and everything to do with me. It wasn't a lesson in praying for healing in someone. It was a lesson in obedience. And I failed it miserably. But God can turn all things for good, and that day, we all learned something.

Months passed, and my second chance finally came. It was a Monday. Jimmy's intervenor called the church office to speak to me and advised me that Jimmy was in the hospital with pneumonia. She said it didn't look good, and he was fading quickly. She thought I might like to know. I thanked her for calling and instantly resolved that I would go to see him. But as the day came to an end, fear had come to pay me a visit, once again telling me that if I pray for him nothing would happen, and why bother? Tuesday came and went. Wednesday, I was determined I was going to go after work. But after work was too late. The intervenor called me to let me know that Jimmy had passed away last evening. I collapsed on my desk. What had I done? I had asked God to give me another chance, and I had blown it, again! I was so ashamed. Jimmy was gone, and I hadn't gone to see him. For a brief moment, the thought passed through my mind that I could go and pray that he be raised from the dead, but fear immediately shut that one down as well.

This story doesn't have a happy ending. It is not one that

shares something amazing that happened or an outcome that was fantastic. This is a story of disobedience on my part, twice. It is not something I am proud of or even wanted to share. But it is a story that will encourage any who have ever been in this position and done the same thing. It is a story that will show that we are all on the same learning journey, and hopefully a story that will encourage you to continue on.

Since Jimmy, my wonderful Savior and King has many times asked me to pray for others, and in obedience, I have. Sometimes with miraculous outcomes, sometimes with no outcome. But He is kind and gentle always. Always there to guide, correct, reassure, and re-point me in the right direction of faith. My prayer for you is that you will continue to pick yourself up when you don't, or can't, follow through. His hand will always be waiting there for you to try again.

Every now and then, when I think of Jimmy, the Holy Spirit reassures me that Jimmy holds no ill will toward me. Jimmy is in his perfect, heavenly body now with his Savior and King, and someday I will get to see him again. I will get to say I am sorry for my disobedience here on earth toward him. But I know it won't matter. He won't care. Thank you, Lord, for your patience, graciousness, kindness, and love, which you continually show to me despite my continuous failings.

Chapter 5

Black-and-White Faith

That fateful day when Jesus walked into my living room and met me, I promised I would love Him forever and follow His every Word. I would follow it black and white, word for word. If he said I could, then I would expect I would. If He said it would happen, I wouldn't doubt. The following are some stories of the black-and-white, no-gray-area-of-doubt times that have happened in our lives.

Jesus in the Meeting

An international healing evangelist was coming within a hundred kilometers of us. We made sure we were sitting in the seats at one of his meetings. As we sang "Shakina Glory Come," I sensed the Lord Jesus walk in. I heard the Holy Spirit say, "Honor the King. Kneel before Him." I knelt down in the space between my chair and the one very close in front of me, with my forehead resting on the back of that chair. I closed my eyes and instantly "saw" Jesus walk in through the door at the front of the room on the left. He was wearing royal garments, including a long, flowing, purple velvet cape trimmed with gold and white. He had on a kingly crown that was four-sided, covered with gold and purple velvet and trimmed with jewels. He held a golden scepter in his hand.

He walked across the front of the room smiling, just nodding at His people worshipping. Then He walked back across the front of the room and bent over and kissed each of the people on the forehead—tenderly, quietly, the way a parent kisses a sleeping child. He walked down the aisle beside me and my husband, kissing each as He went. Then He walked back up the center aisle and went to the preacher. He climbed inside his physical body and disappeared. And then instantly, I saw Him again at the front of the auditorium, with shoulder-to-shoulder angels lined up around the perimeter of the room. Jesus pulled a purple velvet sachet out from under the left side of his cape, reached into it with His right hand, and began to toss what looked like gold dust onto the people in the front rows. He was smiling as He calmly did this. He then turned to the angels on His right and motioned for them to move. The angels then pulled golden watering cans out from under their left wings and began to water the gold dust on the people in the front row. Instantly, huge, thick vines began to grow up and around these people from their laps, entwining them, but not choking them. There were huge, heart-shaped green leaves on the vines.

Then Jesus looked out the windows that spanned the other side of the room, and I looked too. The windows had the faces of gray and black demons pressed against them. Jesus raised His hand. The angels lined up in front of the windows turned around and faced outward, and through the angels, I watched the demons be thrown back violently and melt away incredibly fast, like ink being sucked back into a distant jar. The windows were then clear, and the angels turned back around and faced inward toward us.

I looked at Jesus again, and I saw a shiny, huge sword start coming out of His mouth. It was at least three feet long. He swiftly moved it over people's heads, cutting off something I couldn't see. Then the sword disappeared, and when He opened his mouth again, thick blue water, like a river, began to come out of His mouth. The river gushed forward quickly; it was clear and didn't have ripples or waves in it. The river flowed straight out toward us worshipping, coming through us and around us. I felt wet all over and warm. Full, satisfied, consumed, numb, but fully aware of every sense. This continued throughout the entire song, at least ten minutes.

I stood up and instantly felt as if someone or something had flown past my left ear, in between me and Ryan. It was a fast breeze, enough to make my hair move and every fiber of my being bristle.

There is no great hoo-ha ending to this story. It was just an incredible evening of worship and prayer and being in the presence of God and His people. But being able to see what was happening in the spiritual realm with my physical eyes helped solidify the reality of what happens around us on a daily basis and why things happen the way they happen. I am learning to "tune in and tune up" my spiritual senses, including vision. My inner, spiritual eye saw what the physical eye could not. Jesus there. Always present in our daily lives. Bringing faith down from mystical to child-like—to black and white. He has taught me that everything I do or think, and He is available, just waiting for my invitation to join me. From the littlest things to the ginormous, He cares.

The Jesus Chair

Subject line: "Fw:." *Subject Line:* "Fw:" We all hate them. Forwards. They clog up our inboxes and annoy us with their stupid end lines stating, "Pass this on or your house will explode in twenty seconds" or "If you love me and Jesus, you will send it on and send it back so I know ..." Bah! But we all keep reading them and keep sending them on, just because we can't *not* send them on. Forwards. Ridiculous.

But one forward I received was well worth the read. I am sure that most have gotten this one. I received it for the first time in 2003, and again it came around to my inbox again in 2011, a gentle reminder of a life lesson learned so many years earlier. It went something like this:

> An elderly woman was in the last few months of her life and was bedridden, unable to get up at all. Her children came to visit her daily, and as she lay there, they would talk with her and sing to her. As the days went, on her responses became less and less, until they knew that the end was very close. They called the woman's pastor to come and pray with her. When the pastor arrived, the woman could barely speak or stay awake. During limited conversation, she told the

pastor that she wanted to see Jesus before she died. Did He really hear her prayers? Was He really there? Holy Spirit inspired, the pastor got up, found a wooden chair, and brought it to the side of her bed. He instructed her to look at the chair and envision Jesus sitting there when she prayed. And to no longer pray as a ritual learned, but to speak to Jesus as a friend who was sitting there visiting her. Offering final words of love and encouragement, the pastor departed. Days passed, and the chair remained beside the bed. When visitors wanted to sit there, the old woman fussed and told them not to. When someone wanted to move it, she told the person no. The woman's final day came, and her spirit passed on to Glory. When her family arrived that day to visit her, they found her body on the floor, kneeling in front of the chair. Her arms were wrapped around the seat, and her head was resting on it. The pastor had joined them and smiled when he saw the scene in front of him. The family was alarmed and had no idea why she would be on the floor like that. But the pastor—he knew. He knew the old woman fell asleep in earthly death with her head in the lap of her Savior.

The first time I received this forward, I had been a real Christian for a few short months and was still pushing out through twenty years of false religious teachings. It was like thick mud that engulfed me when I learned new things. I had been taught that eyes must be closed and heads bowed during prayer. A pious, righteous monotone voice was to be used, and you were never to move around. Jehovah was the One we prayed to, and we only used Jesus's name at the end of the prayer: "In Jesus's name, amen." Speaking to Jesus was never taught, and the Holy Spirit was only God's "active force, like electricity." These lies swirled in my head constantly as the light of truth was penetrating from my new learning. The Jesus chair. I longed to talk to Him the way He had spoken to me years earlier in my bedroom that fateful night when I was going to take my life. But I didn't know how. I am quite sure that Jesus Himself sent that forward to me that day. I went to the dining room, got a chair, turned it around, and sat on the floor in front of it. I looked at the chair and imagined my Jesus sitting there. Then I began to talk. And talk and talk. I spilled my thoughts, hurts, and dreams onto the seat of that chair. I talked to the chair for weeks and weeks until something broke in my spirit. The lie-teaching of religious prayer busted apart in my spirit woman, and I was set free! I began to see Jesus everywhere I went. He was always with me. When I needed to talk, to ask a question, to cry, there was no longer a need to find a private place and bow my head; I could just talk! He always heard me. He was always right there.

The Jesus chair found its way into our youth group and home study groups. Each teen would get a chair, spreading out around the room, and sit in front of it. Looking at the chairs, they would ask Him to reveal Himself to them. Whether on the blackboard of their imaginations to see with their spiritual eyes or an open-eyed vision of Him, each and every one could see and hear Him. Sobbing would arise from around the room as one by one, they met their Savior and He melted away their hurts and caressed their dreams. Jesus is more real than the hair on your arms. He is never more than a word away. Sometimes not even that. The Jesus chair teaching allows a human to create an opening in the physical world to tangibly learn how to see and feel God. It is not necessary and by no means doctrine—I daresay many would scoff at me for even discussing such a thing—but it is a wonderful way to open the door between heaven and earth and to say, "Jesus, please come. I want you here."

To this day, my Jesus still has a chair. Or the front seat beside me on the way to work. Or the side of my bed. Some days, I see Him with my physical outside eyes. Sometimes with my spiritual inside eyes. But He never leaves. Each time I call His name, He answers. And I am learning to do the same.

You Have a $0 Balance

When Ryan and I met Jesus, we had thousands and thousands of dollars in debt and many more thousands in collections. Phone calls from collectors were daily conversations, and changing of phone numbers was regular to avoid them. We spent what we made with no regard to paying back what was owed. This seemed to be a regular way of life for most that we knew, and we had the attitude that debt was a part of life and not that big of a deal.

We would sporadically get waves of maturity and make plans to pay things off, but then when something caught our eye that we wanted to buy or dinner out seemed better than groceries, we would give in to that soulful desire. Payday loan institutions knew us by name.

After life together for two years, we were offered the opportunity to purchase the duplex we had been renting. It was very small, in a very bad neighborhood, and was offered to us for fifty thousand dollars. A house all to ourselves with a yard, in a neighborhood that although bad, we had lived in for some time now and it hadn't bothered us? Yes, we will take it! Our landlord recommended a mortgage broker for us to go and see, someone he used regularly and who he said could for sure get us approved for this small mortgage. We called him and made our appointment.

Sitting in the broker's office suddenly brought our foolish choices to the surface as we disclosed our debt to him. As we listed collections after collections, unpaid credit card after unpaid credit card, our fun-filled, soul-satisfying living seemed at this time very shallow and childish. After we had given him our details, he smiled weakly and excused us to a waiting room. As we sat in expectation, we already knew the answer. We knew that as Canadian Tire wouldn't give us a store credit card, there was not a bank in the country that would give us a mortgage.

A short time later, we were called back into his office, where he told us what we already knew. Not only did he tell us that we couldn't have a mortgage, but he advised us to get on a payment plan, pay off all the debt, get a secured credit card or loan to rebuild our credit, and perhaps in five to ten years we could apply again and get approval. Five to ten years before we could buy a house? Defeat in an area is even more reason to sink deeper into it.

Weak attempts to mend our ways on our own proved to no avail. We continued on our path of financial self-destruction. Continued in the mindset of "This is the way it is, and this is the way it is always going to be, and why bother trying? The end goal is so far away we are never going to make it anyway." Self-destruction. The devil didn't have to ruin us; we were doing a fine job on our own.

It was within months that we met Jesus and gave our lives to Him, and He began doing supernatural healings in every area of our lives, including financial healing. Within eighteen months of meeting that first mortgage broker, we attended a John Bevere weekend conference in our hometown. (God bless John Bevere, and thank You for him and his obedience to preach what You told him to!) As fairly new Christians, we hadn't been exposed to very many Christian writers and speakers, and we had no idea who John Bevere was. Our church was advertising that he was coming to a local church and that although his conference sessions during the day had a price, the evening sessions were free. Excellent. We liked free. And at this time in our early Christian walk, we didn't think that preachers should charge for their meetings anyway, so we would go just because everyone else was going too and it was free. What we didn't know was that the free session we were to receive was worth more than the thousands that we owed in debt.

There were three free sessions. The first one began with John stating that he had had something planned to preach on that evening, but Holy Spirit had advised him to preach on something else. John began his preaching with laying an incredible Bible foundation. He didn't use notes, he spoke ridiculously fast, and he had Bible verses memorized from many different translations. He would ask if someone had a particular translation, and then he would ask the person to read it out loud as he quoted it along with the reading. John moved around through the audience, and he knew what he was talking about. This was very different from the Jehovah's Witness meetings I was used to, where the speaker was given an outline and stood still at a podium to read it. John was full of life, John knew what he was talking about, and John was obviously being directed by Someone I knew little about. By the end of that first meeting, John had my attention. I had been an avid student of the Bible in my Witness days and was now sitting under a pastor in our home church who was passionate about teaching it, so the fact that John *knew* the Word inside out gave him credit enough in my mind to continue to listen. He had me hook, line, and sinker.

The following free session was the hammer dropping. The Holy Spirit had told John that our city's unbreakable spiritual ceiling was due to the church's lack of tithing. I hadn't had any deep teaching as of yet on tithing. I knew our church passed a collection plate that we randomly dropped twenty-dollar bills into, and Jehovah's Witnesses had taught me that tithing was a false teaching that churches used to rob people, or "fleece the flock." So my understanding of tithing was very, very limited, and my purse strings were very, very tight. When he began speaking, the religious spirit in me rose up, and so did my back. But within minutes of Holy Spirit-inspired preaching, my spirit woman responded to the truth that was being taught and my spiritual ears opened to receive the light he offered.

Within minutes of that light going off in my head, I began to sob. Sobbing in church had become a regular thing for me in the eighteen months of my new Christian walk, and I knew when it happened that something was going to happen in me. It didn't matter to me that John was publicly and harshly scolding the church body for not tithing. It didn't matter that this was one of the hardest discipline hammers I had ever received in my life. It didn't matter because it was God-inspired and done in love, and all discipline done in love reaps repentance and a new heart from it. When John commanded all to whom this teaching applied to *stand up*, I jumped out of my chair. Big, giant, tall woman sobbing uncontrollably, jumping up out of her chair instantly! I knew very little, but what I did know was that I didn't have a choice. There was no "Well, I guess I should stand up; he is talking about me. I guess this applies to me. Yeah, sorry, God, for not tithing. Okay, fine, I will stand up—but not until someone else does ..." No, that conversation in my head didn't happen. It was more like "Get up! Get up! God is talking through this man right now, and if you are not instantly obedient to this, who knows what will happen? Get up—the God of the Universe is talking directly to you!" I didn't have a choice. It was as if a giant remote-controlled spring was under my seat that threw me out of it. John led us in a very strongly worded prayer of repentance, and then, as if that wasn't enough, he instructed us to come up to the front and line up along the platform. At this point in time, it didn't matter to me why; I did what I was told. But the obedience in moving to the front was not a lesson in mockery or shaming, but instead the second part of discipline: the offering and receiving of love and blessing. When my children do wrong, they are told what they have done wrong, they are disciplined, normally they repent willingly if the infraction is explained clearly, and then they are hugged and hugged and reassured and loved on. And that is what we received when we moved to the front. As I followed the other three quarters of the attendees to the front of the building, the heat suddenly got turned up. By the time I got there, it felt like it was a hundred degrees. But it wasn't temperature heat. It was the heat of His love for us. His presence was so tangible that I felt like I was walking through a midsummer heat wave, one of the kind that you can feel on your skin when you walk outside from an air-conditioned building. It wrapped around me, and I melted. His love on my spirit brought me to sobbing even more. I cried and cried and asked Him to forgive me for not tithing. He understood. As He always does. He said He forgave me, and then he led John to walk along the row and pray for each one of us. I cannot tell you what John said, but I do know that when he prayed for me, it was Dad's love flowing out through him.

As we are one, both Ryan and I got the revelation of tithing that weekend, and we immediately started being obedient to it.

Three weekends after that time with John Bevere and our newfound revelation on tithing, my mom asked if we were still considering buying a home. With an eight-month-old child and living in a top-floor apartment approaching summer, she didn't like the thought of us spending it without air conditioning and no backyard to play in. We explained again our financial situation and what the last mortgage broker had told us, and she asked us to try her bank representative. Mom had just remortgaged and thought we might have a chance. We agreed and made the appointment, but knew what the outcome would be.

We sat at the bank officer's desk, our paperwork in tow. She smiled that condescending, "I feel so sorry for you" smile and said she couldn't help us. Shocker. She gave us the same advice the last mortgage broker had and sent us on our way. One more nail the in the coffin of financial freedom in our minds.

Two days later, she called and said that she couldn't stop thinking about us, and she had referred us to her independent mortgage broker friend. She advised that she had given our information to the broker, who would be in touch within a few days. Shortly after that, the broker called. And the conversation that ensued is one that changed our lives and exploded our faith. The mortgage broker said, "I am the mortgage broker that the bank referred your file to. The bank officer told me that you had this and this debt and this and this in collections, and I have your credit report in front of me, but each debt is showing 'paid in full.' I can see the debts were there, but they are all at a $0 balance, and you both have perfect credit." I gasped. Then gasped again. Then asked her to repeat herself. I asked again if she was sure. She confirmed it. I told her we hadn't paid them. She said that someone had, and she would be able to get us financing to purchase a very nice home. *Are you kidding me? Really?* I fell off my chair, thanked her, discussed the details of the pre-approval amount, and then fell on my face and worshipped my God in heaven, who was faithful! He had said that if I brought a tenth of my earnings into the storehouse, He would open up the heavens until there was no more want! He promised, and He kept it! Three weeks of tithing by faith and a heart full of love, and He fulfilled His promise! Thank you, Lord! I called Ryan, he too fell over, and two months later, we were into our first house.

To continue this story ...

We wanted to live in Henderson Survey. Henderson Survey, in our minds, is the nicest place to live in Brantford. The homes are fifty to seventy years old; the neighborhood has wide streets, huge, mature trees, beautifully manicured gardens, and well-taken-care of homes. The best public school and the nicest parks. Only blocks from downtown and blocks from all amenities. Minutes to the church. But Henderson Survey came with a hefty price tag, and houses there sold within hours of being listed, most listings not even getting signs on the lawn before they were sold. We didn't think we had a chance.

I got the call from the mortgage broker on Wednesday afternoon. I called Ryan on his cell phone on his way home from work. He carpooled with two men who lived in Henderson Survey on the same street. When they pulled onto their street that Wednesday evening, there it was. A house directly in between them, with a "for sale" sign on the lawn! Ryan came home and got me, we drove to the house, and without even going through it, I told him it was ours! I knew in my deepest of depths that this was our house and we were going to get it. We called the realtor and made an appointment to see it the next afternoon. They told us there had already been several showings that day. Thursday took forever to come before we were in the driveway and ready to move our hearts in. We walked through the side gate, and I fell in love immediately. A beautiful, enclosed, tree-covered patio leading to a professionally landscaped backyard surrounded by mature pine trees! I turned to the realtor and said, "We'll take it!" She asked if I wanted to see inside, I said, "Sure, if you feel you must show us, but it doesn't really matter!" (That, of course, entailed a roll of the eyes by my Ryan!) The inside matched the outside in perfection of what we wanted and needed, and we asked to make an offer. The realtor told us the seller wasn't taking offers until Saturday, two days later, as there were several people interested and ready to offer. It was going to be a bidding war. I was more determined than ever now; bring on the competition! We went home and, after praying about it, decided what we would offer. Saturday came. The realtor called and said she was going into the bidding meeting, and a short time later she called to tell us that we were the proud owners of our first house!

A mortgage we shouldn't have received and didn't deserve to receive, a perfect house in a neighborhood that was very difficult to get into, a bidding war with multiple offers. Each of these things in the natural would have seemed insurmountable and would have made most people not even want to try because they would know they would fail. But His promise was that if we were faithful to tithe, He would be faithful to open the heavens. And open them He did. Thank you, Lord, again, for your faithfulness in all things.

Storms and Feathers

Our beautiful house that Father God gave us, on the street we always dreamed of living on, with the mortgage we didn't deserve to have, was surrounded on three sides by hundred-year-old pine trees. They towered above the hydro lines and were bigger around than two people could reach finger to finger. They had stood the test of time. They provided incredible shaded relief from the hot summer sun, bountiful homes for every color and kind of bird you can imagine, and the most amazing canvas for fresh-fallen snow. I loved those trees.

But storm winds do not like tall trees. Trees of that height were taunting to storm winds. They would call out, "Come and find me, blow at me, and see how far I can bend without breaking! I'm right here!" I am quite sure I heard the trees speak to the winds on more than one occasion. This particular evening, a summer storm came up quickly and within an hour was battering our house with rain and pounding the treetops against it. I was in bed and heard loud crashing. Running out the back door, I saw that the wind had picked up our patio table and flipped it upside down, and the chairs were over the six-foot fence and littering the yard beyond. I looked up at the trees through the driving rain. Their tops were reaching their middles as they were tortured and forced to bow by the twisting storm winds. I ran inside and back up to my bed. As I lay there listening to the trees pound the roof directly above me, I initially felt fear. I was alone with my child, as Ryan was at work, and could only think about a tree falling on the house and crashing down on top of us. But then spirit woman Alison rose to the surface and reminded the soul who was in charge. The Holy Spirit brought verses to mind that caused faith to rise up and words of action to be spoken. The Holy Spirit reminded me that Jesus spoke to the winds over the Sea of Galilee and they calmed. The Holy Spirit reminded me that Jesus said that whatever He did, I could do also. He gently urged me to do the same. "Go ahead, speak to the trees. Tell them to stop bending. Ask the Lord of heaven to send His angels to surround the property and stop the wind from blowing over it. Call down heaven to earth." And that is what I did.

Back down the stairs I went, opened the back door, and shouted out into the rain, "In Jesus's name I command the trees to stop moving!" Close the door, back in bed, asked my Dad in heaven to send His angels to surround our property and stop the wind from blowing, so that our house would be protected. Within seconds, the noise of the storm stopped. The battering of the trees on the rooftop silenced. I got up and looked across the street, and the storm was still continuing. The trees on the opposite side of the street were floundering around in the tumultuous gusts, but the tree in our front yard was perfectly still. Not a leaf was moving. Running back outside to the backyard, I saw the same thing. My hundred-year-old pines stood straight up and stately, while the rest of the neighborhood was under assault.

The day after a storm always brings beautiful sunshine, clear skies, and calm. And as I wandered the yard putting furniture back in its place to where it was uprooted from before I prayed the night before, I noticed something. Then something else. Then more and more. As I walked the perimeter of the yard, I found that small, white, downy feathers marked it. A distinct line of angel feathers surrounding the property. A small reminder from Dad above that when we ask, we receive (Matthew 21:22). If we have faith to believe, He has the power and will to send it. Angels are real. Father God in heaven is real. Our words having power is real. We just have to believe it. It was a storm. But I was scared, and it was important to me that the trees stopped swaying. Simple. Not a desperate prayer for a dying child. Not an unrelenting intercession for a loved one with cancer. Just trees and wind. Regular life stuff. Incredibly, the God of the Universe still cares about the simple-life stuff too.

An interesting thing about those trees. We lived in that home for four years, and I prayed continuously that they would never fall on us or our property. Within months of us moving out, three trees came down: one over the fence, destroying the neighbor's deck, and two into the backyard. Thank you, Lord, for your eternal faithfulness to answer when we pray and ask.

No More PMS

Yes, I said it. P-M-S. Every woman dreads it. So does every man who has to be around a woman who has it. I was no exception. Vicious, debilitating abdominal cramps. Crazy lower back pain. Aching thighs, headaches, bloating, and the most horrible of all, the mood swings. The "I am going to kill you now so it be in your best interest to *get out of my face!*" to the "I love you so much I could just eat you up!" swings. The not wanting to move off the heating pad for the first three days of the period to the feeling weak, faint, and malnourished last three days of it. Never knowing when it was coming, never knowing when it was leaving. Period. It sucked.

Then one day, it all changed for me. I met my friend Sue at a wedding. And Sue helped open the door to one more benefit of being under Covenant with our King, one more tidbit of redemption that hadn't yet been brought to my attention. (By the way, Sue and her husband Charlie are two of the most amazing people I know. Check out their website at www.WhyNotCityMissions. com and see why.)

It was a glorious Saturday in June with hundreds of guests waiting patiently for the bride to walk down the path under the fragrant pink blossoms of the cherry trees. The ladies in attendance were all in gorgeous summer dresses and sandals—all the ladies except myself. Sue noticed. Sue came over and inquisitively asked why I was dressed in dark army-green trousers with a tank top, and not in a gown like the others. But she already knew the answer. In her gentle Sue manner, she offered the advice that I no longer was under the curse and I no longer had to put up with PMS symptoms or anything of the like. Jesus's blood had redeemed me from the curse of pain in childbirth, and He had redeemed me from the curse of PMS symptoms. I was now free to celebrate being a woman, free to relish the fact that my body functioned the way it does and that I was capable of bearing children because of the way God had made my body. I, of course, glared at her from my period-induced miserable head, thinking, *Is she insane?*

A very interesting discussion started in which Sue shared her own story. How she and Charlie were so busy at the mission that she absolutely did not have time to be laden down with menopausal symptoms, and she told them to hit the road. She reminded her body that it was redeemed from the curse of sin and that menopausal symptoms were part of that curse, and as such, she no longer had to have them. Sue spoke to her body, telling it to come into alignment with the Spirit of God, and that although it would begin to naturally shut down child birthing functions, it would not bring along with it any of the unpleasant side effects that have become accepted as normal in our society. She explained to me that what society has accepted as normal is not what God says normal is. We have just accepted it, and therefore, it happens. We *expect* it, and our body manifests exactly what we expect it to. After she told her body to come into alignment with the Spirit of God and spoke life over it, the menopausal symptoms went away! Praise God! If we would only read His word and believe it. If we would only speak life-giving words over ourselves and our loved ones, how much better off would we be?

I had already learned that when Sue spoke, I was to pay attention. I went home that evening and asked my Holy Spirit if this was true for me too. Could I really have no more PMS? After twenty years of it, it is sometimes hard to believe. He most kindly told me that yes, I too didn't have to accept these symptoms any more. They were not from God, they were a result of sin, and I was redeemed from the sinful nature. *Okay, here goes nothing.*

It has been several years since that wonderful wedding day in June. And several years of no longer having "normal" PMS symptoms. Along with heeding what I had been told, I took it one step further. I decided I didn't want to have my period on weekends, so not only did I tell my body that it was not going to have PMS anymore, but I also told it that my period was only allowed to come on Mondays, *never* to arrive on a weekend. No more aching back, no more abdominal cramps, no more never knowing when it was coming or how long it would stay. Proverbs 18:21 says, "Death and life are in the power of the tongue. Those who love it will eat its fruit." I am eating the fruit of life-filled words over my menstrual cycle.

Many times when I tell people this story, they think it wrong of me to have done this. They think that we shouldn't expect God's power to take things like this away. That this is a woman's "thorn in our flesh to keep us humble and remember that He is God and one day our bodies will be perfect when we get to heaven." I have even had some people say that it was selfish of me to ask God to take this away. Bah! That's crazy talk! If that were the case, then we shouldn't ever ask for anything, because it is all selfish! Matthew 11:7 tells me, "If you then, being evil, know how to give good gifts to your children, how much more will your Father in heaven give good things to those who ask Him?" If my children are hurting and they come and ask me to help the pain go away, of course I will do whatever is in my power to do that! So why do we think that our Father God in heaven doesn't feel the same way about us? Why do we think we have to suffer on earth with pain? We don't! He has made a way for us to not suffer. We just have to appropriate the gift He has already provided.

No more PMS, no more childbirth pain, no more fear of horrid menopause. No more. I am redeemed by the blood of the Lamb. I am saved by the grace of God. And I am living, walking proof that the power in the blood is not just for eternity's sake, but it is for now's sake. I just have to ask for it.

Your Womb Is Not Empty

In the summer of 2006, Ryan and I traveled with a group of people from our hometown of Brantford to Canada's capital city of Ottawa for a twelve-hour prayer vigil on Parliament's front lawn. We knew the leaders of the group, but no one else. Surrounded by five thousand others, we experienced an incredible day of prayer and blessing on our nation. As Ottawa hotels were packed to capacity, we chose to stay at the Arden Circle Square Ranch, which was about an hour and half drive from the Hill. The ranch was closed for the season, and they graciously allowed our group use of the facilities for the evening and the following morning. We arrived late that night, and after our own time of worship around the campfire, we retired to our dorms.

In the morning after breakfast, we were offered use of the ranch's chapel to have our own worship service. One of the ladies from the group had her guitar and led us in worship and songs of praise to our Almighty King. It was a very informal morning— singing, prayers for each other, and communion. Then, someone whom I didn't know, but who has since become very dear to me, came over to me with a word of prophecy. She walked up to me, put her hands on my shoulders, and looking intently in my eyes, said, "Dear, your womb is not closed. You are going to have another baby."

What? I didn't know this woman from anyone; how on earth did she know that I had been crying out to the Lord for another child? How did she know that I had wanted another baby for over a year now and hadn't been able to get pregnant? How on earth did she know? Because it wasn't "on earth." Her hearing and responding was to the word of knowledge dropped into her from the Holy Spirit about what was "in heaven" already. And as she spoke, I heard and "saw" the name Evangeline. I heard it with my inside-my-head ears, and I saw the letters "E-v-a-n-g-e-l-i-n-e" drop onto my mind's blackboard. As Connect Four pieces drop into the board, *clink, clink, clink,* that is how I saw her name drop into my mind's eye.

Then, as if that wasn't enough, another whom I didn't know, who was on the other side of the room and not involved in this conversation at all, came over, randomly put his hand on my belly, and said, "I bind every word of cursing that has been spoken over this woman's womb and every word spoken by a doctor who said she couldn't have another child. I declare this womb to be open in Jesus name!" and then he walked away. *Whoa!* I was blown away. He hadn't been part of this. He couldn't have heard what the other woman had said over the music and others praying. He had been on the other side of the room. But he too, an obedient friend of Jesus, followed His instructions given by the Holy Spirit and spoke the words he was told. I went home elated, knowing in my deepest knower that despite what the outward physical displayed, my God was faithful to hear my prayers and He would give me another child.

The following November, three months after this prophecy had long faded to the background of my memory, I was led to do a ten-day fast. There was a strong burning in my heart to fast for our youth group and our church. For those ten days, I drank only juice and water and felt fantastic at the end of it. Following the fast, Ryan and I took a week-long trip to the Dominican Republic. A wonderful week of playing in the surf and all-you-can-eat five-star food. My period was due that week, but it didn't come, and I thought it was the Lord's favor on me in holding if off so I didn't have it on our holidays. The following week at home, my period still did not come. I did, however, have lots of brown "spotting," which I thought was odd. *I am now two weeks late for my period that normally comes like clockwork, and all I get is this?* By Saturday, I thought perhaps I should ask the Holy Spirit what was going on with my body. (Duh! Why didn't I ask in the first place? I know. I know.) I asked, and He advised, "You are pregnant." *What?* I rushed to the bathroom to my stockpile of pregnancy tests, and voila! There it was! The telltale double blue line confirming I was pregnant! And as I looked at that stick, her name once again dropped into my head. He once again softly whispered, "Her name is Evangeline."

I dropped to my knees in thanks and worship, and then raced to the living room to explode on Ryan. "Her name is Evangeline!" I cried.

As I had been spotting for a week, we thought it best to go to the doctor to ensure that all was okay. (Yes, a moment of flesh rising up in fear.) It was the weekend, so we needed to go to the hospital. After what seemed like hours in the emergency room, the doctor finally saw me, confirmed my pregnancy, and then said that we shouldn't get our hopes up that my body would "keep" the baby, as brown spotting was indicative of miscarriage. I told him absolutely not, her name was Evangeline, and she would be fine. (Ooo, look! The flesh lay down, and faith was back!) He smiled sweetly and said okay.

The doctor determined my date of conception. It was the exact same date as when our first daughter Genevieve was conceived three years earlier. This was amazing to me. And what was more amazing was that God proved that He was in charge over this little one's life and I had nothing to do with it, as I had *fasted* through her fourth week of life in me and eaten ridiculously on our vacation through her fifth week, followed by a week of spotting dead blood. *He* was in charge. *He* knew her. And there was nothing that would take her away from me.

At month four, I went for my first ultrasound. The technician asked at the beginning of our appointment, "Do you want to know what you are having?"

I smiled and said, "I am having a girl, and her name is Evangeline." He laughed and said that all moms think they know what they are having. I said, "No, I *know*. I am having a girl, and her name is Evangeline. God told me so." This time he just looked at me.

At the end of the appointment of watching my beautiful baby be measured and determined, he again asked, "Do you want to know what you are having?"

I smiled at him and said, "If it makes you feel better to tell me, you go right ahead, but I told you already that I am having a girl."

He laughed and said, "You're right—you're having a girl!"

My God doesn't lie. I know His voice. And when He says something is going to happen, no matter what the earthly circumstances say, His Word always prevails. Five months later, my beautiful Evangeline was born on her exact date she was supposed to come. God's Word prevailed.

No Pain in Childbirth

I became pregnant with our first child shortly before giving my life to my King and Redeemer Christ Jesus. I was desperately hungry for the Word of God and all that I could learn about the truth of Him, and so I attended every ministry group, Bible study, and fellowship time I came across. I read everything someone offered me, spending hours and hours reading my Bible and in prayer. I chose to believe everything I read in the Word, black and white, and assumed that if God would do it for someone written about in there, He would do it for me. I advanced quickly in my knowledge and in my faith.

Around the entrance to my third trimester, a fellow believer in my church suggested that I should begin praying and believing that I wouldn't have pain in childbirth. She recounted her personal story of how she took the Word at face value, believing that she was redeemed from the curse and that she would not have to have pain in childbirth, and therefore, when the time came for the birth of her second child, it took place *pain-free*. I was in shock and disbelief, passed her off as a crazy Christian crackpot, and proceeded to have nineteen torturous hours of the most incredible-screaming-how-could-you-do-this-to-me-I-will-never-do-this-again childbirth pain three months later. Apparently, my knowledge and faith had not yet advanced to her level.

However, exactly three years later, they had. Three years after the conception of our first child, the conception of child number two took place. And from that moment on, my diligence in study and prayer, as well as God's faith-growing in me, took hold. I began declaring to myself and everyone who would listen that not only was I going to have my child at home with a midwife, because *I knew* I would have no complications. but I was not going to have pain either! I was redeemed from the curse, saved by grace, seated with Christ in heavenly places, healed by His wounds, and I was not going to have pain in childbirth! I was never so sure as I was at that time in my life that I was going to speak out the Words of my God over myself and He would ensure that they would come to pass. I was a woman propelled by the desire to *never* again go through the pain I had gone through three years earlier and passionate about demonstrating the promises of Jesus! I was on a mission! I was driven! Isaiah 55:11 states, "So shall my Word be that goes forth from my mouth, it shall not return to Me void, but it shall accomplish what I please, and it shall prosper in the thing for which I sent it." Well, I spoke out His Word over myself and thanked Him over and over again for my redemption from the curse. Galatians 3:12–14: "Yet the law is not of faith, but 'the man who does them shall live by them.' Christ has redeemed us from the curse of the law, having become a curse for us, (for it is written, 'Cursed is everyone who hangs on a tree,') that the blessing of Abraham might come upon the Gentiles in Christ Jesus, that we might receive the promise of the Spirit through faith." I was not going to have pain! I was not going to have pain! And—I didn't.

I had an incredible pregnancy with little discomfort through-out most of it, other than having a child who insisted on practising her neck-strengthening and head-turning skills while still inside of me. Not pleasant. However, on that glorious July 30 morning, at 4:40 a.m., I knew it was time. I was awakened with cramps that

I thought were a continuation of the past three weeks of false labor. By 5:00 a.m., I knew it was the real deal. I woke my husband, telling him to call the midwife and have her come—Evangeline was on her way out. The midwife arrived at our home by 5:30 a.m., and by 6:00 a.m. I was fully dilated and ready to push. With no pain and minimal discomfort on my part, Evangeline arrived on the scene at 6:20 a.m. with the effort of three good pushes. *Pain-free childbirth*. Textbook delivery. Zero complications. My God promised it. I declared and believed it. My body took hold of the promises He offered, and the rest fell into line. What was different from child one to child two? Was my God different? Was His choice to allow me to have pain or not have pain different? The *only* thing different between the two labors, as far as my end of the deal went, was my faith. The first round, I did not have the faith to believe it or the gumption to try. My experience thus far had not opened my eyes to the potential God had for me. I was thinking and living out of a theology filter that said, "That can't really happen. You have never seen a creative miracle; therefore, they don't happen." And although I didn't want to really think that way and somewhere deep down I thought I had more faith, I didn't.

In the three years that followed Evangeline's birth, I dedicated myself to intense Bible study and meditation, as well as a focused side-study on physical healing in our bodies through addressing the spiritual roots of sickness. I surrounded myself with people who fully believed in the spiritual roots of sickness and pain. I studied the writings and journals of great international Christian leaders, who daily moved in creative miracles, overcoming the darkness in their worlds by speaking out the Light of the Word. And my faith grew. And my love of my God grew. And I began to realize that God is faithful. That He is not a respecter of persons. That if He will do for one, He will do for all. We just have to ask. And when it comes to our bodies, we have to take them captive and tell them what they will and will not do! The spirit needs to be in control, not the body.

I learned the power of the spoken Word. "Death and life *are* in the power of the tongue, and those who love it will eat its fruit" (Proverbs 18:21). I *chose* to speak life over my baby and life over my body. "Out of the same mouth proceed blessing and cursing. My brethren, these things ought not to be so. Does a spring send forth fresh *water* and bitter from the same opening? Can a fig tree, my brethren, bear olives, or a grapevine bear figs? Thus no spring yields both salt water and fresh" (James 3:10–12). How can we possibly profess Jesus as Lord and then say, "This is just the way things are; you can't escape childbirth pain—it's the natural part of life"? I think the best line that I heard from a fellow believer was that God *gave* women pain in childbirth, quoting from Genesis, as the person smugly told me that I was going against God's will for women by saying that I was not going to have pain in childbirth. I found that most interesting. My Bible states that Jesus's sacrifice covers all sins, all pain, all suffering. I believe that childbirth pain was included in that. I was right.

We need to get to the point in our lives where we begin to believe the Bible as it is written and stop reading what we believe. When we cut out the gray area and the options for interpretation and just *read it*, it is amazing what begins to take place in our lives. My second child's delivery is living proof of that.

My Big Toe

For as long as I can remember, the big toe on my right foot would poke up and cause holes in my runners. When I was a tween, the canvas Bi-Way white tennis shoes were all the rage. My mother would get so frustrated with me because within weeks of getting new shoes, I would have a hole in the right toe. They wouldn't even be dirty yet, but there was the hole. Every pair of tights, panty-hose, and socks felt the oncoming doom of the inevitable big-toe damage. The nail chose to grow up at an angle, instead of growing flat and straight out like normal toenails. Thus the holes. They started out little, but then with wear, they got bigger and bigger until my big toe was naked and screaming, "Look at me!" from every pair of socks and slippers I donned. In desperation, my mom found "toe socks," little tiny single socks the size of, and made specifically for, my big toe. To wear under my foot-socks. Like little tiny toe girdles. They didn't work. My toenail wore through the tiny toe sock and found its way out of the foot-socks and shoes.

My dad had the irksome big toes too. Only his weren't so pretty. His nails not only grew up, but were thick and yellow and bumpy too. They caused him great pain, so much that he inevitably ended his toe misery by having the nails removed from both big toes. In my teenage years, mine didn't cause me pain and weren't overly ugly to look at, but by the time I hit twenty, the nail began to grow thicker and always had white powder under it that smelled oh-so-wonderful. I learned that this nail had a fungus. I began doing foot soaks and prescriptions and whatever the market could sell me that promised an end to the fungus. I soaked it in medicine, in lemon juice, and in Listerine, all in hopes that the promises made would come true and the end of my toe misery would be in sight. To no avail.

I began always having to have nail polish on my toes to hide the yellow hue my nail had taken on. By the time my first daughter came along, the toe was constantly infected and swollen, so much so that if I stubbed the end of it, green infection would ooze out of the corner of my nail bed. Gross.

A year before my daughter was born, I met my Jesus. Within weeks of my meeting Him, He healed all the major chronic illnesses that plagued me—all but this one. And I had become so used to it, having had this irritation most of my life, that I didn't think to ask for a healing of it. Three years later, when my second daughter was born, it had become very, very irritating. All shoes bothered it. Stubbing it was excruciating. Having my now-three-year-old step on it would almost make me pass out from the pain. I was done with this nonsense, and it had to go.

At this time, I had also begun an in-depth study of the spiritual roots of sicknesses, focusing my main study on the works of Pastor Henry Wright (*The More Excellent Way*). I was learning that there were spiritual roots to most chronic diseases. I prayed over my toe, told it to be healed in Jesus's name, and anointed it with oil, but I saw no changes. The classic church excuses of, "Well, maybe that's your 'thorn in your side,'" or, "It will be healed in God's timing,'" or "You don't have enough faith," or my personal favorite, "If God wanted it to be healed, He would have done it by now," continuously were in my head. I was tired of praying for it and nothing happening; I was tired of wondering why it wasn't better. I gave up. I relented to the "if God wants to heal it, He can, because I am tired of asking" mentality and stopped asking for it. Really stopped thinking about. Until the next time I stubbed it. Or Genevieve stepped on it.

Then we met another amazing group of people who loved God and knew His power and understood that He *never* doesn't *want* to heal something. They understood that there was something else that needed to be addressed before the healing could come.

My husband and I were invited by our amazing friend to her grandparents' home for a barbeque and social time with some of her friends and family. We had met none of the others before, but were always up for a good time with good food, so of course we said yes! As the meal came to an end, a huge storm was brewing and forced us to come indoors. We gathered together in the basement for "home church." All we had ever known of God's power and awesomeness was revamped that evening. All the ideals we had ever seen and participated in for worship were broadened by pure, undiluted, from-the-gut worship from believers who didn't need music or prompts or cues to sing out to their God.

Our friend's cousin took charge and led our group time, beginning with singing out songs that we knew. He would pause, another would begin singing, and the rest would join in. Then he stated that the Lord was going to do some healing tonight, and if anything popped into anyone's head, then we should just speak it out. I wanted my toe healed but absolutely did not want these strangers viewing it, so I determined right then that I would not ask anyone to pray for my toe. My Lord, of course, had different plans. And He had believers surrounding me who knew His voice and who would pay attention when He spoke. A few minutes went by, and I clearly heard the words *heel spur* pop into my mind. I thought, *Hmm, I don't have a heel spur, so someone else must have one, and then no one will pray for me, and I won't be embarrassed.* So I waited for a pause in the singing, and I said, "Heel spur. Those are the words that popped into my head." The leader thanked me for sharing and asked who had the heel spur that needed to be healed. No one. No one responded, and I immediately began to feel quite silly.

Then he said, "No, wait. This happened for a reason. Does anyone have any ailment on their feet at all? How about something wrong with a big toe?" Busted! Tricky-tricky our God is! *He* knew that if He told me to speak up about my big toe, I wouldn't because I would be too embarrassed around these new friends, so He had me speak out about a heel spur so that it would come back around to me! I sheepishly put my hand up and admitted I had the toe issue. The leader asked one of the others, who worked in the medical field, to come and pray for me. Within seconds of her coming near me, I involuntarily screamed, my body slid forward off the chair, and I slithered under it like a cartoon person who was flat. Slithered the way a snake would. It was the "demonic snake" inside of me that knew its time was up because the believers on the outside shone Jesus. It saw the power of the Lord coming toward it with the pending prayer of faith that was going to come out of the woman who prayed for me.

The next few minutes of dialogue included the new friends asking me if anyone in my family had this toe fungus, to which

I replied, "My dad." They prayed and declared that that generational curse was broken in Jesus's name, not only over me and my toe, but over my family and the generations to come from me. I was led in prayers of repentance for my own sins and prayers of forgiveness toward others, and it was declared that my toe was healed in Jesus's name! My toe tingled for the rest of the evening, and I felt the sensation of minty coolness all through it.

As I lay down to sleep a few hours later, I thanked my Lord for healing my toe. I knew it was done. I knew it was better. And as I prayed, He took me into a vision that was so real I thought it was really happening. It was as if I was looking at my big toe, seeing it beautiful and normal and the nail white and smooth and pretty! I was so excited that when I came out of the vision, and realized it was a vision, I looked at my toe expecting it to be perfect as I had seen it in the vision. But it was still thick, yellow, and ugly. I consoled myself and said that when I woke up, it would be all better. And when I woke, it wasn't. And for the next week, I faithfully told my toe that it was healed, and I spoke to it and told it to be pretty in Jesus's name, and so on. I told everyone that my toe was healed and that God had moved miraculously in my toe, thinking that if I spoke out the truth that I knew was on the inside, then the outside would have to follow through. But it didn't. And the days turned into weeks and the weeks into months. And all that changed on my big, giant, gross, painful big toe was that the nail stopped growing and it got yellower. I lost hope. I lost faith. This big-toe dilemma dominated most of my prayer time and my idle thinking time. A toe. How sad is that?

Then one Sunday morning five months later, as I was getting

out of the shower, my towel caught on the corner of my toenail, causing me excruciating pain. When I hobbled up the stairs to my bedroom and sat down on the floor for an inspection, I began to see something. This old, gross, yellow nail was pulling away from my toe! I thought, *Oh no! I don't want to be nail-less like my dad!* If there is something grosser than the thick, yellow nail, it's the no-nail look of the big toe. That was even uglier! As I inspected further and tugged a little at the nail where the towel had caught, I realized that the only thing that was holding this nail on was my cuticle. I pulled down the cuticle from the sides and the bottom, and voila! The old nail popped right off! And underneath—the delicate, thin, white, smooth, pearly beauty that I had seen in my vision months earlier! The beautiful new was there all along! I just had to pull the old off to see it.

How much of our lives are like my big toe nail? Yellow and ugly and smelling horrific, but we put up with it because we think we have to? Because we think that's just the way it is, that's the way it's always been, and that's the way it will always be? How many of us pray and pray and declare and bind and thank and curse and continue on without looking at what the root of the issue is? Whether it's for a healing in body, an issue in a relationship, or a job we would rather not have, everything has a root, and if we deal with the root, then the plant will have to change. My Lord told me my toe was healed that night. The root was dealt with—the generational curse of the spirit of Infirmity was bound and cast out, and there was nothing left that would *legally* allow that disease to continue in my toe. It was then declared that the new nail would come to fruition, which it did, that night. My Lord then *showed* me the new toe in a vision that night. What more could He have done? He could have made the old nail morph into the new right in front of my eyes; that would have been cool. He could have made the old nail fall off right there, so I could see the new underneath; that would have been great too. So why did I have to wait five months before I could see the new nail? Why the torture of making me think that it wasn't healed and that it didn't really happen? Why the continued anguish?

I asked Him. And He, so gracious and gentle, explained to me His wisdom in it all. By allowing me to continue with the old nail on top for five months before seeing the new one, He elevated my faith in more ways than ever would have happened had any of the fun, cool things mentioned above taken place.

He taught me to believe the vision. Had I come out of the vision on the night of the prayer, looked at my toe, believed the vision, and started picking at my nail, I would have seen how He uses visions to show us what has already taken place in heaven and bring that heavenly perfection to earth. I know that now. When He gives me a vision and tells me it's for right now, I now understand and further the discussion by asking, "What do I need to do to bring that heavenly vision to earth right now?"

He taught me to never accept what I see in the natural to be what the reality is. That the supernatural reality is what I should always be looking for, not just taking what I see in front of my physical eyes to be real. Had I believed the supernatural reality of what He had shown me and told me through the faithful prayers of my new friends, then I wouldn't have allowed myself to go to sleep without pursuing Him and finding out where this new toenail was.

He taught me that many times I accept the uncomfortable, the irritating, and the *common* as normal. My dad had the toe fungus. Apparently, some of my grandparents did too. Possibly their parents too. Accept it. It's hereditary. You know what word I have come to hate since becoming a Christian? *Hereditary.* Hereditary sicknesses are a crock and a lie from the pit of hell to keep people in bondage to sicknesses and diseases and continue the curses from generation to generation! Most "hereditary" diseases are rooted in spiritual issues that can be broken by faith in the sacrifice of Jesus's death on the cross and believing His Word over the lies spoken by the enemy for the past hundreds of years! I refuse to come under the *hereditary* diseases lie and have broken those curses over myself and my family for the generations to come! I will not, nor will my children or grandchildren, suffer from osteoarthritis, diabetes, cancer, toe fungus, alcoholism, blood disorders, depression, or anything else that has plagued my family in prior generations! By allowing the old toe to stay on with the new toe firmly planted underneath, my gracious God showed me that I have to *do* something to walk in the perfection that He offers to me here on earth. He did His job. He gave me the new nail. I had to do my part. I had to pull that old nail off.

Our God does His part, and we do ours. If I don't like my job, I can pray and fast and ask and beg and get all the intercessors at my church to pray for me too that I will get a new job. But if I don't go out and apply for one, I won't get it. If I don't get qualified for the position I desire, I won't get it. If I don't prepare for the interview and plan for it, I won't do well. We do our part; He does His part.

If I don't like how my children are behaving, I can fast and pray and pray some more for Him to fix them and beg and yell at them and scold them and continue doing what I have always done, and nothing will change. But when I seek Him, ask His counsel for what *I* have done to induce the behavior they are giving out, and change how I respond to them, then He can wipe away the old, ugly behavior to reveal the true, desirable behavior underneath. I do my part; He does His.

He also taught me that when we live with things for so long, we begin to think they are normal. I no longer want normal. I want what I read in the Bible. I want to walk in perfect health and offer perfect health to everyone that I meet by offering them Jesus. I don't want to be sick. I want to have my shadow fall on others and for them to be healed because the power of the Holy Spirit is so present on me. I want to see into heaven on a regular basis, be transported as Stephen and Paul were, physically see angels and chariots of fire as Elijah did, and move in every miracle that every believer has moved in since Jesus was resurrected to His heavenly throne thousands of years ago, and more. I want to pick up serpents and have their venom not hurt me, drink poison and have it not kill me. Do I sound off my rocker? Do I sound abnormal? Good. No more normal. No more ugly, yellow grossness hiding my heavenly perfection. When I say my children are capable of doing something, I only say it if I truly know they can do it. They have faith in me that I wouldn't lie to them. They know that if Mom says they can, then they can. My Dad in heaven is the same. He says I can; childlike, black-and-white faith agrees. The experiences He has graciously given me are living proof of that.

Chapter 6

Pursuing Greater Gifts

There are diversities of gifts, but the same Spirit. There are differences of ministries, but the same Lord. And there are diversities of activities, but it is the same God who works all in all. But the manifestation of the Spirit is given to each one for the profit of all: for to one is given the word of wisdom through the Spirit, to another the word of knowledge through the same Spirit, to another faith by the same Spirit, to another gifts of healings by the same Spirit, to another the working of miracles, to another prophecy, to another discerning of spirits, to another different kinds of tongues, to another the interpretation of tongues. But one and the same Spirit works all these things, distributing to each one individually as He wills ... Do all have gifts of healings? Do all speak with tongues? Do all interpret? But earnestly desire the best gifts. And yet I show you a more excellent way.

—1 Corinthians 12:4–11, 30–31

I wanted it all. I heard people speaking in tongues, and I wanted to too. I heard people offer words of knowledge over others, and I wanted to too. Visions? I wanted that. Anointed dreams? Yes please. Gifts of healings, workings of miracles, prophesying? Could I have it? Okay, I wanted that too. Why? To bring heaven to earth. Moving in the supernatural became all I could think about. It wasn't that I wanted to do these things for my own glory. I wanted to do what I read about in the Bible. I wanted to show the world that the real Jesus isn't religion and pious door-knocking, but He is alive and well and cares about our world right now as it is. That His power and health and love are accessible right now. And being able to move in these supernatural aspects would show that to the world. My Jesus knew my heart and my desire to serve Him with everything that was available, and He began to send down the gifts.

Speaking in Tongues

Our beautiful home church in Brantford was filled with many, many amazing people. Within weeks of beginning to go and then meeting Jesus, we joined everything we could. We enrolled in the Alpha Program, went to the youth nights, and joined home groups. We couldn't get enough of this new kind of love that we were receiving from our new family. Most were reserved and prayed in the way I was used to hearing: "Dear Father, thank you's, pleases, in Jesus's name, amen." But there were a few who muttered under their breaths words not understandable. Some talked crazy fast in what sounded like gibberish, while others repeated the same sounds over and over again like a skipping CD: "Du-du-du-du-du." Upon asking what this was, I was told it was speaking in tongues. Growing up as a Jehovah's Witness, I had been told that this was demonic and that true Christians did not do this. Only those Christians who were present at Pentecost in the upper room were granted that gift, and any who said they did it now were apostates. It was drilled into me that those who said they did it were possessed by demons. Repeated teachings stick, whether true or false, so when I heard my new family members doing this, it made me uneasy. As time went on, speaking in tongues was explained to me repeatedly, and I studied my Bible for myself on the topic. After much research and prayer, I realized that it was a gift from God, it was still relevant today, and it was something that I should be asking for. Praying in tongues became all I could think about. I wanted it more than anything else.

Two years after becoming a Christian, I began praying with my two neighbors. On our first meeting together that wonderful November morning, both immediately began to pray out loud in tongues. While one of us was praying in English, the other would be praying out loud in tongues. I found it a bit unnerving and asked the Holy Spirit what was going on. He explained to me that they were not being disrespectful and "praying over me" but were praying alongside in their spiritual language. I didn't tell either of them that I hadn't been blessed with the gift yet, but I didn't need to. By Thursday of that week, one randomly said to me, "You will be blessed with the gift of tongues. Do you want it?"

"Of course I do!" I said back.

She prayed a short prayer over me asking the Lord to pour out the gift of tongues on me, and then she told me to start speaking. Nothing happened. She smiled and said, "It will come."

That evening was FaithWorks school. Intense Bible training with curriculum from Hillsong Church in Australia. What was the topic? The Holy Spirit and the gift of tongues. I went home that night with my head spinning about what I was learning. I told my Lord that I wanted tongues so that I could pray for others when I ran out of words in English. When I didn't know how to pray for someone, the Holy Spirit could pray through me for them. I wanted it! I wanted it! I wanted it! Ryan was on afternoons, so I had the late evening to myself. I typically spent this time in intercession before going to bed, and I began going through my prayer list. When praying for others, I always pray out loud, so I began to speak. Within seconds, my tongue started bouncing in my mouth. First a little, then a lot. Then it began flapping around in my mouth uncontrollably, bouncing from cheek to cheek, roof to bottom! I began gargling and making bizarre sounds. I thought in a flash, *God, is this tongues?* It was scary and bizarre, so I screamed out, *"Stop!"* It stopped. My heart was pounding as I gained control of my tongue. My head was spinning as to what this was. If it was tongues, would I feel scared? Would I lose control of my mouth? I didn't think so. It didn't make sense. I said in my head, *If this is you, Lord, and this is how it works, okay, I will do it. But I am not comfortable with it—in fact, I am kind of scared.* I relaxed and opened my mouth. Within seconds, my tongue began flapping inside again, this time violently. My jaw rocked from side to side, and then I felt what can only be described as a snake sliding down the inside of my throat, but a snake with hands that were grabbing the walls of my throat on the way down and closing it behind itself. I screamed out and told it to stop in Jesus's name!

Petrified, I called one of my spiritual sisters. Before I could even tell her what had happened, the Holy Spirit told her, and she prayed out forcefully that whatever demonic thing was doing this in my body was to leave in Jesus's name! I felt the snake come back up my throat. I heaved as if to throw up, and I felt it physically leave my mouth. My friend prayed with me to ease the fear as I crawled back into bed, watching the clock till Ryan got home. That was the last time this ever happened, and that ended my asking for tongues.

The next morning, my neighbor asked me if I wanted to speak in tongues that day. I told her no and told her why. She explained that the devil would always try to counterfeit God's gifts and with this gift, to counterfeit it so I would be scared and not do it or ask for it again. She advised that when He was ready for me to have the gift, He would give it and it would come with peace. I, however, stopped asking for it and tried to stop thinking about it. Another week went by, and the following Thursday night after FaithWorks, I again retired to my bed for my time of intercession before Ryan got home from work. As I lay in my bed, I began to go through my prayer list. Once it was finished, I asked the Holy Spirit whom He wanted me to pray for. I was instructed to intercede for all the Jehovah's Witnesses that I knew. As I began to do so, words I didn't understand started to come out. I instantly was praying in a language that I had never heard before, but in my head, I knew what the words meant. As I prayed in this new language, my voice became louder, I spoke faster, and the power of heaven surged through my body like never before! Images of Witnesses that I knew flashed in my mind, and I knew I was praying for them, my ears not understanding the words but my heart knowing what was being said. There was no fear, no trepidation. I knew that this was real, and this was the Holy Spirit working through me—*this* was tongues!

First Corinthians 12:31: "But earnestly desire the best gifts." I earnestly desired this gift. It was granted and now used for His glory and purposes through me. I have met many Christians who do not speak in tongues. Some don't believe in it, thinking as Jehovah's Witnesses think. Some think it is a gift for some and not for others, and because they don't do it, then it must not be for them. Others have said that they don't want it because they think that it is demonstrative and showy and not necessary. I have even had some people, including church leaders, say that they don't want it because they think it will make others feel uncomfortable around them. My Bible says for me to earnestly desire the best gifts. It also says this is a gift from God. It was a gift to the first Christians at Pentecost, and it has been a gift to millions of Christians since then. My God is not a respecter of persons; therefore, what He will give to one, He will give to any who ask of Him. As for it being demonstrative, there is a time and place for everything. Discretion and asking for the Holy Spirit's direction in every movement of the Spirit are required at all times. Let

Him tell you when it's okay to speak in tongues out loud or when under your breath is more appropriate. Let Him tell you who will be offended by it and whom it really doesn't matter if you offend. But it is a gift, one we are told to earnestly desire.

Black-and-white faith told me that if one could have it, I could too. Black-and-white faith told me that if the Word says it can be bestowed upon me, then it would be if I asked. The day I said yes to Jesus, I also said that I would believe every word of His Bible, front to back, cover to cover. I wouldn't interpret it to fit my preconceptions, and I would do whatever He asked of me. He planted in my heart the desire for the best gifts, He nurtured those seeds of desire in my heart through others around me, and when the time was perfect, He allowed the seed to rupture and root the plant inside. I am forever grateful that the Holy Spirit has chosen to dwell within me and forever grateful that my God would trust me enough with this most precious gift. But the desire hasn't stopped there. I will continue to desire the "best gifts." Not snippets of them here and there, but daily walking in *all* the spiritual gifts of heaven for His glory here on earth until the day He takes me home. If you know Jesus as your Lord and Savior and you do not yet speak in tongues, ask Him. "If you then, being evil, know how to give good gifts to your children, how much more will your heavenly Father give the Holy Spirit to those who ask Him!" (Luke 11:12–14).

And Visions

> And it shall come to pass afterwards that I will
> pour out my Spirit on all flesh, Your sons and

> Your daughters shall prophesy, Your old men
> shall dream dreams, Your young men shall see
> visions.
>
> —Joel 2:28

I have always had an active imagination and was vivid in my descriptions of everything. But the first time I had a heavenly vision, I was undone. We had been Christians for a very short while, and my knowledge of gifts of the Spirit was still incredibly limited. I had read about a few international spiritual giants who talked of visions regularly, but I didn't think that this kind of blessing of heaven could be received or given to regular Jane mommies whose daily activities consisted of diaper changing, feedings, and naps. Again I was proven wrong. Again my Jesus showed me that "simple and regular" equalled perfect in His eyes.

The worship band began to play "Here I Am to Worship." As it was the song that was playing when Jesus walked into my living room that incredible, life-changing day, each time I heard it, I melted. We were sitting in the middle section of church, and I was a sobbing mess. Hands raised in adoration of my King, I began to see the back wall of the church morph into Calvary Hill. Purple-orange storm sky, dirt and dust blowing everywhere. I saw hundreds of crosses on the hill, each with a death-sentenced criminal hanging on it. The picture grew clearer as it seemed to get closer and closer to me. I then recognized that the cross closest to me had *me* hanging on it! A God-sized hand came out of the sky. With two fingers, it gently plucked me off the cross and gingerly set me down on the ground. The rest of His body appeared out of the darkened sky and shrank to my size. He then climbed up the cross and took my place on it. That moment in time, I realized the entire spectrum of what Jesus did for me that horrific day in history. Sobbing uncontrollably, I heard Him say, "I want you to go up to the front and share with the congregation what you just saw." I couldn't. I was so new in my faith, so scared of what others would think of me, so afraid of being embarrassed, I couldn't. Gentle and patient, He said, "You have asked to see visions. I have given you one. Gifts of the Spirit are for the purpose of edifying the church. This will edify the body. Should you not share and grow what you have been given, even what you have will be taken away." *Done. I'll do it.* Up I went, interrupted the band, and asked to share what I had been given. Little did I know what edification given at the exact moment it is commanded from heaven could do to a group of hungry believers whose hearts were ready to receive it. Big giant God, regular-Jane mommy, a little bit of courage, and a whole lot of motivation equalled an entire church transformed by one vision of heaven. Simple. We get so caught up in the human-driven technicality of it all. Jesus lived simply when He was on earth. He slept. He prayed. He preached. He chilled with His friends and hung out, eating and drinking. He lived life simply but still for the sole purpose of bringing the kingdom of heaven to earth and proclaiming the name of His Father. When we can get ourselves and our own hang-ups out of the way and simply say yes to whatever He asks of us, all heaven can break forth from our obedience.

I was invited to speak at a women's breakfast at a local church. It was a fabulous morning of great food and great friendship building. Seventy-five women from the congregation had gathered to enjoy each other and to worship our God in a united voice. The chairs had been cleared from the sanctuary and circled round the breakfast tables at one end. That left the entire middle section open for free movement during worship. There were no chairs to line up behind, no taped lines on the floor signalling where we should stand. But by rote, the women began to form lines near the back of the room, standing side by side, not spacing out to enable dancing or flagging or anything else. The worship leader invited them to come closer to the stage, to spread out, to relax and feel free to move as they were so led. A few shuffled a bit closer but did nothing of any kind of significance. The band began to play, and the voices were muffled, each afraid that the others would hear them and no one wanting to stand out. One or two picked up flags and waved them gingerly, but the rest remained chained to the floor behind their imaginary pews. Chained to their perceived ideas of what worship should look like. Chained to fear of what others might think of them.

I was immediately taken into one of the most vivid visions I had had up to that point in my Christian walk. I was transported into a massive, massive corridor. The floors were made of gleaming marble. I could feel the cool luxuriousness of the tiles beneath my feet. Although I was aware that I was still in the warm, carpeted sanctuary, my feet were bare and relishing the smooth floor below. The corridor was thirty to forty feet wide, and the ceiling soared above me. It was rounded and painted with the most glorious murals of beauty. Along each side of the corridor were round-topped openings. Each was lined with massive marble columns reaching to the ceiling above. I at first thought that they were windows, but after looking further, I saw that they were openings to the vastness beyond them. Each opening was flanked with orange-and-gold-and-red curtains. The material looked like the finest silk and were solid but translucent at the same time. A gentle breeze blew from the left to the right of the corridor, whisking the curtains back and forth into it. They were gorgeous and drew you into them, like silk sheets that you just want to dive into and never come out of. Along the middle of the corridor was a red carpet. It glowed and moved with the breezes.

Expanding my gaze down the corridor, I saw that at the end of it was another round-topped, massive opening. Soaring columns flanked either side of it. And there, in the middle, He sat. I saw my Jesus. Sitting on His throne, smiling at me. Although He seemed to be a great distance away that might take me minutes to get to, I could see Him smiling. He held a golden scepter in His hands, and after a quick glance to his left, confirming with Father His next action, He extended the scepter to me. I knew from study that when a king extends his scepter, it means an invitation to approach the throne. Without that invitation, a subject could be condemned to death. Instantly, there were angels at my side to escort me onto the red carpet. Softness like I had never felt before under my feet when I stepped onto it. Then, without any more steps taken, I was at the end of the carpet and in front of my

King. Words of love poured from me; words of love poured from Him. He told me to tell the others in the room of what I had seen and tell them that they too were welcome; all they had to do was close their eyes, and he would bring them in. He instructed me to interrupt the worship band and invite the ladies to join me in the throne room. Lead them into the vision by telling them what I had seen, and as I spoke, He would meet them and the vision with their spirits would become their own. By this time in my Christian walk, obedience no longer took two or three requests from my patient Holy Spirit; it was instant.

I snapped back into the physical and did as instructed. I asked the ladies to join me there. And as I spoke and described what was right in front of them waiting for them to walk into, the ceiling of self-consciousness broke and love poured out. Weeping began throughout the gathering. Ladies began to fall to their knees in adoration and pure worship. Others picked up flags and danced wildly. Some began to receive words of knowledge for others; one received a prophecy for that church body, which she delivered with such vigor that it brought us all to crumbling. As the band played on, an incredible freedom in worship was released. "Enter into His gates with praise, His courts with thanksgiving" (Psalm 100:4). From that day forward, I did. From that day forward, as soon as I begin to worship, I am in this place, entering His gates and courts with thanksgiving and praise.

Three years later, a pastor friend was sent an incredible picture. He was so excited about it that it became the backdrop to his church projection screen. He was telling Ryan about it and e-mailed it to him. Ryan called me into his office wanting me to check out this incredible picture that Pastor had e-mailed him. It was the throne room, the very same place God had taken me that morning three years earlier. The center hall corridor, the rounded roof, the soaring columns on the side—in a beautiful photograph with a bride standing at the end, ready to walk toward her groom seated at the other.

Have you been there? Ask Him, and He will bring you in. And on the outside, you will never be the same again.

An Everyday Sunday

Tears with Names

> You number my wanderings, put my tears in Your bottle, are they not in Your book? When I cry out to you, then my enemies will turn back, this I know, because God is for me.
>
> —Psalm 56:7–9

Church began this Sunday like any other. Greeting friends, talking about our week. But when you ask how someone is, sometimes you have to be prepared for the answer that may not be "fine." Upon my asking her the question, my friend exploded with tears streaming down her face as she spoke of the pain that was upon her. We hugged and prayed and talked and hugged some more. Worship began, and we remained arm in arm as the Holy Spirit comforted her in her troubles. As we sat there and the music continued, the Holy Spirit asked me to look up at her. In her tears,

He let me see something. As each large tear rolled from her closed eyes, I saw words in them. *Pain, fear, hurt, sin*—each written in the tears as they rolled down her cheeks. He told me that as my friend unloaded her hurts onto Jesus's shoulders in silent prayer, He released that very thing in a tear. Each tear held each item she had just spoken to Him. Philippians 4:6–7 states, "Be anxious for nothing, but in everything by prayer and supplication, with thanksgiving, let your requests be made known to God, and the peace of God, which surpasses all understanding, will guard your hearts and minds through Christ Jesus." As my beloved friend released her prayers and supplications to Him, His peace rolled down upon her and purged the hurt inside through the gateway of her tears.

Angels and Fireballs

Worship continued, and with my physical eyes closed, I saw through my spiritual eyes angels outside the ancient stained-glass windows of the building, holding glowing fireballs in their hands. The fireballs were alive and moving, not growing in size but not extinguishing either. The face of each angel was turned upward toward heaven, as if waiting for a signal. And a signal there was. I opened my eyes and saw fellow worshippers randomly putting their hands up in the air. Each time someone did so, an angel would nod, as if accepting instruction from the Leader, and then throw the fireball at the person holding up a hand. Once the fireball was received in the hand, the recipient exploded in worship and dance, or fell prostrate on the floor in adoration of the King.

I raised my hand and also received the flaming live fire of heaven. As it hit me, my body rocked under the power of heaven from within it. I then realized that the band was singing a chorus with words that said, "Come be the fire inside of me." We asked, and He answered. How many times do we sing songs like this and not have any idea of the reality of what we are asking?

Heart Transfusion

In the blessed peace of intercession, worship, and dance, amidst the chaos of drums, electric guitar, and the united chorus of worshippers shouting their exultations to their King, He entered the room. I watched through my spiritual eyes My King descending down into the sanctuary, from larger-than-life to life-size, coming through the ceiling, down from behind the band, and walking off the platform to the main hall. He walked over to where my friend and I were sitting, placing His finger to His lips, motioning me to *Shhhh*. He went to my friend as she wept from her heart, and He reached His hand into her chest and started massaging her heart. As I watched through my spiritual eyes, He smiled at me, pulled His hand out of her chest, and touched the tip of my nose, the way a dad does to his little girl in affection. He then jammed His hand into His own chest and pulled out His heart, reached back into her chest, pulled her heart out, and replaced it with His. His heart started pumping in her body, and then His blood transfused into her body. Heart transfusion. Blood transfusion. One life for another. In that moment of time, I had an incredible realization of the true experience of the cross and what it means in our lives.

That if we choose to do so, His heart can replace our own. His blood sacrificed for ours. We can live on this earth as He did. Doing what He did. Loving the way He did. His part is finished. Our part is the surrender.

Pool of Siloam

After some time, Jesus moved back to the platform and ascended to ceiling height, suspended by His own power and glory. As He opened His arms wide, His glory shone out from His being and poured out on our little congregation. It became blindingly bright to me, with the heat of the Glory enrobing us. While worshipping, I was compelled by the Glory light to move from my chair to the center of the church floor. I needed to—I had to—be in the middle of that light! As soon as I reached the center, I was unable to stand and collapsed to my knees. Through open spiritual eyes, I saw water begin to flow from Jesus and form a pool in front of me on the carpet. It formed a pond enclosed by unseen boundaries. I heard Him say it was the Pool of Siloam. He beckoned me to come into it, indicating that He would heal the pain that I had in my abdomen from an earlier injury. Instantly, as I moved on my knees into it, the pain in my belly ceased, and I was overcome with the heat of heaven inside. I collapsed on my side and then rolled onto my back, unable to move again for minutes. I felt light. Heavy. Drunk. Sober. Melted. I never wanted to move again if I could help it. This feeling of euphoria was better than anything I had ever felt before.

My Jesus told me that we all could experience this. That His sacrifice on the cross was complete for everyone. We just had to appropriate it. We just had to move into it by faith. This was a typical Sunday. This was simple. A group of people, so insane-looking to others but simple to them, in love with their husband in heaven. Having the line between earth and heaven, physical and supernatural, shattered, leaving the two worlds open to meld into each other by faith. Simple Faith. Black and white. No room for gray. No necessity for it. Just a desiring of the greater gifts.

Chapter 7

The White Picket Fence

I saw a war zone. It was hazy with dust, gray and brown as far as the eye could see. I saw bombs going off and landmines exploding. The sky was dark with smoke and moving with masses of demons. There were people running every which way and demons flying above them, throwing hand grenades at them. People were trying to escape, but there was nowhere to go. As I looked to the left of my field of vision, I saw a tall chain-link fence with barbed wire circled on the top, like you would see around a jail compound. In the fence was a gate that had no lock on it. The gate led to lush greenery and peace on the other side.

As I looked at the fence, I saw multitudes of people trying to climb it. They would get part of the way up, and a demon would come and pull them off and throw them back into the dark and dust for torturing. Others would fall off in the climbing, get up, and try again, only to continue to fall off from exhaustion. Some would get to the top but either shred themselves on the barbed wire at the top or fall off in the climbing over. Some did make it over. But they were almost dead from trying and had very little energy to enjoy the life on the other side once they got there. It took them a long time to recover. Very few, if any, saw the gate. But there it was. Ground level, swinging out. I started yelling at the people on the fence to get down and run to the gate. It was large and visible for all to see. It wasn't hidden. But only a few here and there went through the gate. Many saw it and stopped in front of it, but then ran past it and began climbing the fence! I didn't understand. If there was a gate that took them through to the other side, and it required no effort to go through it, why would they still be trying to climb the fence?

I looked far beyond the other side of the chain-link fence, and what I saw was almost indescribable. Lush, green, rolling fields as far as the eye could see. An extraordinary large fruit tree in the middle of the field, with red fruit so large on it that the branches of the tree were hanging to the ground. The entire expanse was breathtaking. The fields brimmed with color, life, and promise.

On the immediate other side of the chain link fence was a green strip of lawn, perhaps twenty to thirty feet wide. It ran the length of the chain-link fence. Beside the strip of lawn, there was a ditch that had wild overgrowth in it, but was not so overgrown that it was too cumbersome to traverse. Beyond that ditch there was a white picket fence, the kind you would see in front of a suburban home, the kind that makes you smile and want to walk along it to peer into the gardens beyond it. It was more decorative than purposeful, and low enough that it could easily be stepped over. Past that beautiful picket fence was the rolling expanse of fields and the tree.

As I looked back to the chain-link fence, I saw large groups of people lingering in this green strip of lawn. I saw easy chairs and big-screen floor-model TVs. People were eating and drinking and enjoying themselves. There was much hoopla and excitement in this crowd as they congratulated themselves for making it over the fence. Many groups of people were gathered together partying in different areas of the lawn strip, and very few seemed to notice that beyond the ditch and the white picket fence, there was green and lushness as far as the eye could see. It was like they saw what was right in front of them, and they stopped looking any further. Those who did see beyond the fence chose not to speak of it to the others and continued in their partying instead.

Looking further down the chain-link fence to the where the gate entered the green lawn strip, I saw a huge, towering white cross. It was directly opposite the gate. As I watched the people who did come through the gate, all stopped and looked at the cross. Some wandered around it, took pictures of it, touched it, and gazed in wonder and amazement, like it was a tourist attraction. Many pulled out lawn chairs and sat in the shade of it. Some, as they came through the gate, glanced at it but then looked over at the people partying in the lawn strip and walked over to join them, completely ignoring the cross. After a time, some who had wandered away to join the parties came back. They looked at the cross, pushed their way through it, struggled through the ditch, climbed over the picket fence, and tiredly walked into the fields, away from the chain-link fence. Some walked through the cross but then wandered back to the easy chairs and TVs. Then there were those who were in the parties and didn't even acknowledge the cross, but after noticing the beautiful fields beyond the picket fence, decided they were going to go there. They went through the overgrowth in the ditch but couldn't for some reason make it over the picket fence. As hard as they tried, they couldn't lift their legs to get over. Something that looked very easy they were unable to do on their own.

Then there was another type of people. These were very few who, immediately after coming through the chain-link gate, ran straight at the cross and *into it*. They were immediately pulled through it and launched over the ditch, over the white picket fence, and into the green fields beyond. As I watched them land in the fields, they lay down and rested. I could see the fear, anxiety, and exhaustion wash off of their faces. And then *He* came. From my vantage point above the chain-link fence, I could clearly see Him. He was beautiful. Glowing in a long, white garment, His hair and beard white as snow, His eyes gleaming the most amazing blue, He walked toward the weary travelers and sat beside them. He picked up each head and gently placed it in his lap. He stroked their foreheads and whispered obvious words of tenderness to them. After a time of rest, the two would get up and walk hand in hand to the tree, where he would ask them which piece of fruit they wanted. He would then pick it, polish it to a shine, and hand it to them for eating. I watched the pair walk hand in hand toward the horizon, never to be seen again.

The peace that overcame me as I watched the scene unfold beyond the white picket fence was a peace I had never felt before. It was a peace that, once you had, you would do everything in your power to never lose.

I looked back down at the chain-link fence. People were still partying on the lawn, but they didn't have the peace that those in the rolling fields had. Although they were no longer in the war zone, struggling to stay alive while fighting off demons of death, and although they were seemingly safe and secure, well-fed, and enjoying life, in each of their faces there was the telltale sign of worry—worry of thinking that this time of peace might end. Worry of thinking that they needed to enjoy every moment they could before this time came to an end. And end it did.

As I watched the partying, the chain-link fence suddenly had a massive roll-up garage door in it. The door rolled up, and demons flew into the lawn and snatched the unwary ones who were standing right by it. They grabbed them from behind and flung them back into the dust and dirt of the war zone behind them! Even worse, those who didn't get snatched didn't even notice that their friends were gone! They didn't notice the roll-up door or the demons behind it. Those who were taken were thrown further back into the war zone than they ever were before. Some lay down defeated and allowed the demons to bludgeon them to death. Some chose to fight, battling their way back to the fence. If they made it to the fence, they continued to try to climb over it, not noticing the gate. They kept climbing and climbing, getting caught up on the barbed wire on the top or falling off onto the dirt below before they even got to the top. Struggling and struggling, they continued to climb, having demons grab their backs and hurl them to the ground. I jumped down from my vantage point in the vision, ran to the gate, and started calling to those climbing, "Come here! Come to the gate! Come walk through it instead of climbing! You don't have to climb! Stop climbing!

Stop climbing!" Very few heard me. Of those who did hear me, less than half came. They chose to struggle on their own over the fence instead of going through the gate. Each time they got caught by a demon, they were thrown further and further back into the war zone, further and further from the fence. I tried to tell them to come to the gate, but they wouldn't. I tried to tell those who were relaxing on the lawn by the fence to move away, to go through the cross and beyond the picket fence, but they ignored me. As for those who were trying to climb over the picket fence without going through the cross, I tried to tell them they couldn't, but it was to no avail.

At this point, my vision changed from a vantage of me watching something unfold to me actually being *in* the vision and being *part of it.* The reality of it was as if it was happening to me in the natural, and my physical body and senses responded. I ran through the gate, through the cross, and was supernaturally launched into the green, lush field. It was softer than brushed wool to lie in. The smell of fresh, green grass and sweet meadow flowers filled my senses. My mouth watered as the scent of the fruit from the tree wafted toward me on the warm breeze. And then I heard footsteps. Footsteps of my Bridegroom coming to collect me. Anticipation of meeting Him caused my heart to beat wildly in my chest. I could smell His sweet aroma as He got closer and closer. I looked up into His eyes when He arrived, and the piercing blue saw right through me to the utter core. In an instant, all shame and fear melted under the power of His love. He took my hand, and the power of the God of heaven coursed through my veins. As we walked hand in hand toward the tree, He read my thoughts and warned me not to look back at the others. He knew and understood my concern for them, but advised that all would have the opportunity to come. Some will come His way. Some will struggle on their own and make it, but be tired at the end. Some will try to come without doing it His way and fail, and some will not come at all. But all that I was to be concerned with now was holding His hand and walking over the horizon into eternity of life. He consoled me that all who chose to either come through the cross immediately and be launched over the picket fence, or those who took their time and did it their way and made it over, would never have to worry about the darkness that they had come from on the other side of the chain-link fence. But as for those who stayed in the lawn along the edge of the chain-link fence, some would be fine, but most would not. Most would get caught when the roll-up door opened. Most would die in the battlefield. And each of them would be completely unaware of the danger they were in.

When I came out of this vision that Tuesday afternoon, my head was spinning. I asked the Lord to explain what I had seen, what it meant, what I was to do with it. This is what He told me.

The war zone is life completely separate from God. Whether humans realize it or not, they are constantly being attacked by the devil and his demons, who have the sole intent to murder them forever. Many humans choose to stay in this war zone and invite the demons into their lives through their lifestyle choices. Others are in the war zone because of their initial placement in life, their spiritual generational curses, and so on. However, no one has to stay in the war zone. There is an escape.

The chain-link fence is the attempt that humans make to

better their lives. It could be improvements through careers, education, and increased finances. It also symbolizes all the things humans do to try to satiate their souls, whether it is drinking, drugs, sex, food, shopping, fitness, gambling, etc. Overall, it represents everything humans strive for and put effort into to make themselves better, or feel better, and to escape the unseen and unknown onslaught of darkness.

The gate in the chain-link fence represents the open and easily accessible invitation from the God of heaven Himself for life eternal in peace. The open door that leads to His Son Jesus. The easy confession that Jesus is Lord. That's it. It's free. It's accessible. And it's open to all who want to come. All can see it; all know about it. Many stop and look at it. Many walk on past without giving it a second thought. But it is there, always standing open.

On the other side of the chain-link fence is the green strip of lawn representing religion in general. Whether those there have truly accepted Jesus as their Lord and Savior or not, they are still on this side of the chain-link fence. Life is just better with "church" in it. This part was interesting to me, and I questioned the Lord when He advised me of this. I said, "Lord, those who didn't pass through the cross and just walked past it and are partying in the grass by the fence—they are not really Christians, are they?" He then showed me that this expanse of lawn right by the chain-link fence represented churches. There are many people who attend churches regularly who are not truly saved. They haven't passed their lives through His cross; they haven't accepted Him as Lord nor truly confessed from their hearts that He is, but they are in the House, and therefore have some protection from the war zone of the enemy. But it truly is a false sense of protection, because as they choose to not make a visible stand for Him and pass through the cross, they stand teetering on the edge of safety under His church's roof and in danger of being caught away by the enemy.

On this expanse of lawn, the cross and the benefits of it are always visible. Everyone knows about Jesus and the power of His sacrifice for their lives. But for those who stay on the expansive lawn, the church in general can become very comfortable, like being in an easy chair. Involving oneself in church activities, ministries, fellowshipping—all of these things can take the place of self-life denial and walking oneself through the cross. It can lead to a life of complacency and blindness to the reality of the danger one may be in.

Matthew 12:43–45: "When an unclean spirit goes out of a man, he goes through dry places, seeking rest, and finds none. Then he says, 'I will return to my house from which I came.' And when he comes, he finds it empty, swept, and put in order. Then he goes and takes with him seven other spirits more wicked than himself, and they enter and dwell there, and the last state of that man is worse than the first. So shall it also be with this wicked generation." In the chain-link fence was the roll-up door. This symbolizes the final moment when the spirit returns with seven others and the final fate of the man is worse than it was in the beginning. The roll-up door! The evil spirit returning and bringing seven others! If we choose to hang out in the hoopla of the church but never really pass through the cross and enter into His rest, we are figuratively sweeping the house clean and then leaving it wide open for the enemy to come back and fill again!

The big-screen TVs? Welcoming the enemy into our lives through media, whether it be TV, radio, movies, social media, fiction, the Internet—anything that glorifies the devil and not Jesus—unlocks the deadbolt and loosens the chains on the rollup door, until *bang!* The door rolls up, and the enemy snatches us. Not only is he allowed to snatch us because we have welcomed him to, but he does it with the strength of eight. As a large terrorist group overtakes their victim, so great is the force that the unwary are thrown back into the darkness, and to a much further distance than they have ever been before.

The cross? It's the cross of Jesus's crucifixion. It represents who Jesus is, what He did for us, and it is also the representation of laying down one's entire self and giving one's life solely to Jesus for His purposes on this earth.

The ones who treated it like a tourist attraction equal those who talk a lot about Jesus, the Word, and miracles. They talk. They talk and talk and talk but do absolutely nothing other than that. The sacrifice He made has absolutely no impact on their lives because they have done nothing other than talk. They haven't truly asked Jesus to be their Lord and Savior, they haven't repented of their sinful lives, and they haven't allowed the power of His sacrifice to change them or save them. They just talk and continue to live their lives as they were before they heard about Him. They may go to church; they may call themselves Christians; they may even preach the Word, but the Word has no impact on them because they haven't laid down their selfish desires and asked Him to be the God of their lives.

The ones who pulled out their lawn chairs and sat in the shade of the cross? Those represent people who understand Jesus's sacrifice, and love the benefits of it. They have confessed Him to be the Christ and have their "ticket" out of hell, and that is all they are concerned with. They are not being tortured by demons, and that is good enough for them.

Beyond the lawn strip was the ditch with slight overgrowth. This represents the final shedding of worldly ways, thoughts, and tendencies. If you have ever stopped on the side of the road on a beautiful summer afternoon to feed horses grazing near the fence, and had to walk down and then back up a ditch to get to them, you know that traversing a ditch is not difficult, but it does take a bit of effort. If the ditch has some bulrushes or wild grasses in it, it takes a bit more effort. Philippians 2:12 says we "work out our salvation with fear and trembling." The ditch represents this.

After the ditch was the white picket fence. The homestretch before the finish line. The welcoming sign of coming home. Picture your favorite movie with a classic suburban location: colonial houses with red doors, foundation gardens brimming with roses, a winding path leading from the house to the sidewalk, and the white picket fence outlining the front yard. As you meander down the sidewalk holding your ice cream, your hands follow the up and down of each picket until you get to the gate that is never closed and creaks softly as it blows back and forth in the summer breeze. A picture of peace. An international symbol of welcome. The white picket fence. Pristinely painted and stately in stature, but ultimately serving no purpose other than decorative. It doesn't keep out intruders; it is not difficult to climb over. But once on the other side of it, a sense of calm, of safety, and of *home* fills your senses. This is what the white picket fence in the vision represents: home. Once over it, you are home, and unless you choose to cross back over it and walk into the war zone, you will always be safe and protected.

Over the pickets, you are now in His care, resting in His bounty of life and abundance. The soft, green fields ready for harvest as far as the eye can see symbolize heaven on earth. Symbolizing everything a human could ever need. Rest, peace, and contentment for the soul and spirit. Physical sustenance with no fear of lack. A horizon line that seems to go on forever—eternity with God Himself.

Red fruit? The extras. Jesus Himself asking what *you* would like to have. The fruit represents the spoils of the earth. "The wealth of the sinner is stored up for the righteous" (Proverbs 13:22). We don't have to be content with just sustenance and basic necessities of life. That is a religious lie. But just as parents want their children to have extras—that new doll, that new Lego set—our Father in heaven wants us to have the desires of our heart as well. He wants to spoil us with extra goodies, just as we want to spoil our own earthly children. There is nothing better than Christmas morning when my girls open the presents that contain the gifts they have been asking for and asking for for the past three months! The squeals and giggles that come from them make it all worth it. Most of the time, it is something very similar to something they already have. It definitely is not something they need, but they just *want it.* And as a parent, I love to give it to them. Daddy in heaven is the same. He just *wants to* give it to us. He wants to watch us enjoy that extra. That's why He made the extras—so His children who love Him and adore Him and follow Him could have them! Religion teaches that the extras are just for the world that spits on Him and despises Him. Does that make any sense at all? No! He created the extras for His special chosen ones, His Church, His Bride. Beautiful red fruit. Red fruit symbolizing the epitome of harvest and bounty. For us.

Have your fingers trailed along the pickets? Have you passed through the gate and walked hand in hand with your Savior to the fruit tree?

Chapter 8

Jesus in Me

Our church had an overseas student intern who had come back to visit for a while. One Sunday morning, she led me in a calm prayer that turned my eyes inward to my soul and brought forth one of the most vivid supernatural experiences I have had yet.

The intern reminded me that the "kingdom of God is within me." She had me rest my palms on my belly, and then she led me in a prayer to once again ask the King of the Universe to come dwell within. She instructed my spirit woman to look within my body, instead of outward, and see what the Lord would do. At that very moment, it was like my physical eyes turned a complete 180 degrees and I was looking inside my physical body. I looked down my insides and saw my muscles, veins, blood vessels, bones, and the inside of my skin. I saw my skin on the outer wall, with a space in between it and my muscular being. This space is where my soul was housed. I knew it was my soul as it moved effortlessly in the space in time between my skin and inner body.

I heard Jesus knocking at my belly from the outside. My soul said, "Come in," and at that moment, I saw Jesus's leg come into my body and slide in beside my soul, between my skin and my inner muscles and bones. Then his other leg came in. Then His arm. And then His head and shoulders as He manoeuvred the rest of His spiritual being into my physical body. I *saw* Jesus's spirit man inside my body, side by side with my soul, in between my skin and my muscles.

The sweet intern then encouraged me to ask Jesus to join my soul. As I did, His Spirit- body became liquid and began wrapping slowly around my soul. His was like a liquid gold that wrapped around my grayish vapor. As it wrapped around, it moved faster and faster, until His liquid gold being was weaving in and out of my gray soul vapor. There soon became no distinction between my soul and His. It was like His spirit then became solid inside my body, and I saw His formed feet push out the bottom of my legs and fill the space where my feet were. His arms stretched into my arm skin, and I saw and then physically felt His hands move into my finger spaces. I saw with my inward-facing eyes His head coming up my neck and into my brain space, and then His head became mine altogether. When He opened His mouth inside my body, my mouth opened. When He flexed His fingers inside my body, my fingers flexed. When His feet moved, so did mine.

There is an incredible song that says, "Where you go, I'll go. What you say, I'll say. What you pray, I'll pray. What you pray, I'll pray." That song became real to me that day. Jesus took over my body. He took over my feet, my hands, and my all. I feel Him inside me. All the time. Not just when someone speaks a prophetic word over me. Not just when there's an anointed worship song on. He's there. Tangible. Real. I feel His hugs from the inside. I hear

His love poems whispered in my ears, more clearly than if He were standing beside me in person on the outside and speaking into my physical ear. He asks us to be His hands and His feet. I now understand what that means.

Worship with Cheerleaders

My daughters attended a girl's club group that is run by a local church in our hometown. On the first night as I was dropping them off, the Holy Spirit asked me to ask the group's leader if they needed any more volunteers. She exclaimed yes and asked if I was volunteering. Yes, yes, yes I was. Then the next week, I was asked by the leadership team to be the club's creative worship leader. Wowie wow, now that is a huge responsibly, huge. I quickly asked the Lord if that was what He would have me do, to which He instantly responded yes. After much discussion between me and the leadership team, it was determined that I had free rein to do as I pleased and as the Holy Spirit led, and that I would rotate between the groups each week, teaching—whatever. Well, that *whatever* turned into the Holy Spirit having a heyday with each group every week! With each week that passed, it just got better and better!

One Particular Evening with the Ten- to Twelve-Year-Olds

Each week, I prayed and asked the Lord what He would like me to do with the group for the evening. He never told me until the drive home from work on the evening of club. I think that if I knew too soon, then I would try and *Alisonize* it, and Holy Spirit wouldn't get center stage, so it was a very big waiting game for me. But a fun one at that. That night, He showed me that we would sit in a circle holding hands, I would put on the hymn "How Great Thou Art," we would worship as a group, and then the Holy Spirit would lead us into "free worship" after that. I was to teach the girls the difference between individual worship and corporate worship, discuss the power in corporate worship, and then head into it.

We sat in our circle, opened in prayer, and turned on the music; then the Holy Spirit took over. By the end of the song, even the shyest of girls were belting the song out from the depths of their hearts. When the music was over, we sat in silence. Then one of the girls began tapping out a beat. Then another. And another. Soon there was a crazy beat that was rising and rising! I got up and began to stomp a crude type of native dance, and then I broke into the song "The Enemy Has Been Defeated." The girls joined in. Then others began to dance. Some stomped, some skipped, and some "Biebered." The other adult leader started singing "Alleluia." So beautiful and powerful and graceful and moving. Other girls joined in with her. I started spinning and spinning and going crazy fast. Then I hit the floor. It was like a jackhammer came out of the sky and knocked me down. I couldn't move. The power of the Holy Spirit on me was like I was being smothered in a hundred-pound, soaking wet blanket of warm love. Girls were singing, yelling, screaming in worship and warfare. Minutes later, I was able to lift my head and saw half the team was on the floor under the power of His presence.

Then the other leader yelled out that we were to open our mouths and let the Lord fill them. *"Open* your mouth! Let the

Lord fill it!" she shouted over and over again. One child said she tasted grape juice in her mouth. Another tasted bread. Still another said she felt like words were put in her mouth. She tangibly felt it. The Holy Spirit moved in me to tell them that Jesus is the wine! Jesus is the bread of life! Jesus is the Word! It was crazy! We kept singing and dancing. I began singing "Let It Reign," and some joined in. Then three girls began singing a song I didn't know, but the presence of the Lord around them was like a thick, dewy fog. As they sang, more joined them. The ones that didn't sing were marching in the middle of the room saying, "The sheep, the sheep, the sheep know the voice of the Shepherd." Over and over again, they marched and chanted. I continued to sing my song, the group continued to sing their song, the chanters kept going, and our precious Holy Spirit sang with us. I could feel Daddy smiling. I could hear Jesus saying, "They're *my* girls. Look at them." The ones who weren't singing or chanting were face-down on the floor, hammered under the power of God's presence.

After a few minutes, the Holy Spirit directed me to Psalm 94:1–6. I was to corral the girls, and we were to each get our Bibles and read with conviction and power those verses. We got our Bibles, we sat down to read, and something happened. The Holy Spirit welled up in me and decided that it was time to instruct the girls in Matthew 10—that they would heal the sick, raise the dead, cast out demons. The fierceness that He spoke through me to them was enough to make me drop to my knees. They were instructed in the power of speaking the Word out, that if they allowed the Holy Spirit to take them over and allowed Him to use them, they would change the world. How speaking God's Word out over something was like God Himself speaking out of their bodies. Then, out of nowhere, joy came in. Joy. Uncontrollable giggling, laughing, snorting, rolling on the floor. Within seconds, we were all in hysterics under the power of God's Joy. We couldn't stop laughing. I was sitting on my knees when we started, and suddenly I flew backward, literally, and was on the floor rolling! So much fun! The girls were going crazy laughing under the power of the Holy Spirit!

A few more minutes passed by, and I heard the Holy Spirit say, "Now it's time. Read out Psalm 97 together." But I thought, *No, that can't be you, Holy Spirit—look what's happening in the girls. They are still under the power of Joy and still laughing. I don't want to stop this.* Wrong. I Alisonized it. Within seconds, one of the girls was walking around reading out loud Psalm 97! I wasn't obedient, and it was required right at that moment in the spirit realm, so He asked her to do it instead, and she was obedient! Humbled? Absolutely. Quickly repenting and confessing to the girls my error? Immediately. Corralled the girls again, told them what had just happened, confessed my disobedience and the young girls' obedience—lesson learned. Lesson taught.

It was at this time that I noticed a tween rubbing her eyes. Both of her eyes were very red and looking swollen. She had a wet cloth and was dabbing and rubbing at them. I asked her what was wrong, and she stated that it had just started a few minutes ago. After a bit of discussion as to what it could be, we determined that it was a spiritual attack that the enemy had sent on her to stop her from being part of this worship time. Another tween volunteered to pray for her, and after a short, sweet, to-the-point, full-of-faith prayer, the itching and pain had instantly gone away! Hallelujah! How awesome is our God? We all then got up, stood in a circle with our Bibles, and very aggressively read out loud together Psalm 97:1–6. So powerful! We said our final prayer for the evening, and the planned time was finished. But the Holy Spirit was not. One of the girls had brought her Justin Bieber CD, and she asked if we could listen to the song "Pray" on it. We popped it in, turned out the light, and danced and sang our hearts out. As parents arrived to gather their girls, the other leader turned the lights back on. And there in the middle of the floor were five of the tweens on their knees, hands clasped tight in front of them, praying and thanking God for the night! Ooo, my mommy heart was warmed!

But wait! There's more! One of the teen boys came in afterward, and he mentioned that his foot was injured and his shoulder hurt. Well, were we going to stand for that? Were pain and suffering allowed in our classroom? Absolutely not! I asked which one of the girls was going to take what they had been given tonight and go and pray for him. One volunteered; she went and simply prayed that his pain would go away in Jesus's name. I then asked him if it was gone. He said kind of. *Not good enough.* She prayed again. Then looked at him. He paused, and then stated that yes, all the pain was gone completely! Praise God!

As a leader, my heart soared watching these incredible young women grow in their faith, understanding, and knowledge of God. As a mother, my emotions raced with love and pride and adoration seeing their spiritual eyes, ears, and hearts be opened to know the love, touch, and voice of our Lover and King Jesus.

But as a fellow worshipper, I was overwhelmed at the honor and privilege that I had of joining this amazing group of believers as they no-holds-barred offered their sacrifice of worship to their God in heaven! If we as adults could be so open and willing to try new things, so ready to trust when someone else offers us a new way of doing, so believing that if we truly *believe,* what we ask will come to pass—then the world would change. The kingdom of heaven would come to earth.

When I first took that position of creative worship leader, I thought it was for the purpose of what I had to offer them, what I could teach them. I now know differently. It was more about, and had always been about, what my God would teach me through those girls. I learned and re-learned what raw, childlike faith is. I was reminded of "first love" feelings and rushes and highs. And I was moved more than ever to love freely, as those girls loved. Thank you, my girls, for all you have taught me. Thank you for your easy belief. Thank you for your openness to try. Thank you for allowing me the privilege and honor of being part of your journey.

Jesus asked us to be His hands and feet. That wonderful season at Girls Alive, I was able to do so.

Snowbank in Heels

We had a past habit of living beyond our means. A mortgage, two car payments, and lots of wants equalled big monthly bills, leaving little left for things like groceries. I can get to the grocery store, and I will look good doing it in my pretty car, but I don't have any money to buy anything. A vicious cycle of bad habits. One particular freezing cold day, while I was on maternity leave and heading to the grocery store with the last hundred dollars I had for another two weeks, I saw a couple walking down the street. They were carrying grocery bags already full and were burdened under the weight of them. As I drove nearer to them, the Holy Spirit told me to pull over and give them all the money I had; they needed it for groceries. *What? But that is all the money we have, and we don't have any groceries in the house, and they are already carrying their groceries; they don't need any more!*

I heard Him again: "Give them all the money you have in your wallet."

Okay, I will do it, but I won't like it. Jesus's hands were on the outside; I was still working on getting my heart on the inside to match.

Quickly, I pulled off to the side of the busy four-lane road with a three-foot-high snowbank butted up against my driver door. A quick adjustment in parking, and now I had about six inches to open my door and get out without being creamed by passing rush hour cars. As I stuck my foot out the door, I looked down at my feet. Knee-high stiletto-heeled boots, meant for pretty, not for traversing frozen-over, dirty snowbanks. Up I went, calling out to the couple for them to stop. I must have been quite a sight. Ridiculous boots, skirt, and a fancy car coat chasing them down the sidewalk. "Here, God told me to give this to you. He said you needed it for groceries," I mumbled out to them while gasping for air in the frigid afternoon gray. When I handed them the money, they looked at me in disbelief. Again I stated that God had told me to give it to them for groceries. They looked down at their hands full of bags, as did I. I didn't understand it; neither did they. But it didn't matter. All that mattered was that Jesus asked me to be His hands and feet that day by filling a need that I didn't know anything about.

Jesus in me—a catchy song, a creative hashtag, words easily spoken but rarely thought about thoroughly as to what they really mean. Of all the daily doings of life, Jesus has taught me that it's when I just *do* what He asks at that time, no matter how silly or insignificant or ridiculous it may seem—like climbing a snow-bank to give money for groceries to people who to my physical eyes don't look like they need any more groceries—*that* is when I am being His hands and feet. Ego requires seeing the fruit of our prayers, the big numbers in the ministry meetings, and the hands raised at salvation calls. A heart bent on just being Jesus to those we meet doesn't need to see the fruit of the effort or even the reason for the effort in the first place; it just desires to be obedient. That is all I want too.

Chapter 9

The Faith Portal

"The biggest personal faith portal in your spirit will always be the area where you have the least amount of faith. Let go of your unbelief in that big area that I am challenging you on, and it will become the biggest direct portal from heaven to you for faith to pass through. It will become the biggest reservoir in your entire being where faith can reside and grow."

During our corporate worship and prayer time at church one Sunday, we were all relishing the presence of our Almighty Father when His Spirit said the above to me. He prompted me to speak it out. I in my arrogance was thinking about the others sitting in the room; knowing some of their struggles, I was thinking that the profound words the Holy Spirit had spoken to me would surely uplift them, encourage them to repent of their unbelief in those areas, and move them in faith to fulfil the challenge the Lord had offered them, whatever it was. However, as the words passed off of my lips, He ever so kindly and gently said, "Those words are for you, daughter. *You* need to let go of your unbelief. *You* need to move in faith in the things I have told you you are to do. *You* need to allow that faith portal to be filled with faith and not unbelief. *You,* daughter, not them."

Aghh! Always. Always me thinking I am on top of the world, and then realizing that once again, I am not. There is always somewhere else to go, something else to do. I am never finished growing. Never finished learning. What is the faith portal blocked by? What is my faith reservoir contaminated with right now? At the time that He spoke those words to me, my lack of faith was in believing that I was a writer. Lack of faith that I could publish a book. *Who would want to read something I have written? What do I have to share? Who really cares what has happened in my life in the past ten years? To me it is pretty awesome, but would anyone else really think so? He* thinks so. He asked me to begin to write a book about His awesomeness in my life over the past ten years. He asked me to do it four years ago. I started. Then I stopped. Then I started again. Then I stopped. Then there were always excuses, always reasons not to, always something that stopped me from doing what He had asked me to do. Why? Bottom line, my lack of faith. My lack of confidence in myself. And that is it, right there. I am nothing without my God. All my confidence needs to be in Him. It is when I get my focus off of Him and onto me that I shut down and stop believing. *He* told me to write a book; I think He knows what is going to happen. I think He knows how it is going to get done. And I don't need to know right now. All I need to do is write. What is your faith portal?

Neighbor Prayers

We had moved into our first house together in the neighborhood where we had always wanted to live. It was an established area of fifty- to eighty-year-old houses, tree-lined streets, wide, grassy boulevards—and it was a very difficult area to purchase a home in. When they came up for sale, normally a sign didn't even make it onto the front lawn before it was sold. Our God blessed us, and there we were. Our neighbors were friendly, and apart from a few "trouble" houses, the street was quiet. One gorgeous fall Sunday afternoon, while my Genevieve and her daddy were napping, I was reading Beth Moore's *Believing God* book in the rocker on our front porch. Beth in her incredible teaching style was encouraging the readers to step out of their comfort zones and do what the Lord was asking of them. I had only known my Jesus for just over a year at this time and was learning to decipher His voice and be obedient when I knew it was Him. I set down the book and asked Jesus what He would like me to do for Him. He promptly responded with, "Go down the street, introduce yourself to Nicki, and state that I want you and her to pray together each morning for one week. You are to pray for the neighbors and the surrounding neighborhood, intercede for the city, and then pray for the nation. Each morning before school for one week. After speaking with Nicki, you are to come back up the street, go to the other end, and introduce yourself to Nancy and tell her the same. Whose house you meet at doesn't matter, just that it gets done." I knew that Nicki was the children's pastor from another church in town, and I knew where she lived, but we had only met one time before in passing. We were not friends, nor were we even neighborly, as she was about ten houses away. Nancy went to my home church; we had smiled at each other every now and then, but again, we weren't friends and didn't really speak. I, however, didn't care. I didn't care what they might think of the stranger coming to their door to announce that God had told me that we were to pray together. I didn't care if they thought I was weird or bizarre. It really didn't matter to me. My God had asked me to do something, and I was going to do it. Faith portal opened. Scary, but open nonetheless.

Immediately, I got off my chair and marched down to Nicki's house. I introduced myself and proceeded to explain what my Jesus had requested. Nicki, being the God-fearing woman that she is, promptly said, "Of course! If Jesus told you that, then we will, and we will start tomorrow." We made arrangements to meet at her house in the morning, and I marched back up the street to Nancy's house. She too offered the same instant response. And so began our six-month journey of meeting together to pray and watching our city, and ourselves, change in response.

That first morning, I hiked my sixteen-month-old toddler down the road at 7:45 a.m. to start what would become one of the most amazing prayerfests of my life so far. The three of us went into Nicki's daughter's bedroom, closed the door, and let the Holy Spirit take the reins. Nicki and Nancy began praying in tongues, which I had yet to do, and I stood there stunned. They then began round-robin praying for the neighbors they knew by name, praying that God's will would be done in the house across the road from Nicki where crack cocaine was being dealt, and for an open heaven over our city of Brantford. By the end of the week, we had fallen into a great routine of prayer. We had also begun to stitch the fabric of a lifetime of friendship, and through our obedience to open our mouths, we began to see changes on our street. At the end of that mandatory week of prayer, we all agreed we didn't want to stop, and we continued to meet for the next six months. Within two weeks of our first meeting, the police raided the drug house; it was cleaned out and ready for sale. A couple who were headed for divorce announced their staying together. The health of an elderly man took a sudden turn for the better. Neighbors who hadn't spoken for some time had made amends.

Within a month's time, we asked our Lord if there was anything he would like us to do together as a group. We all heard that we were to host a street Christmas party, inviting all the neighbors from Nancy's house at one end down to Nicki's at the other. It was five weeks until Christmas, so we knew we had to get ourselves organized for planning. The Holy Spirit directed us in everything that we were to do, and by the end of the week, it was all planned and invitations had been delivered. On the day, everyone on the street except three houses came. Most of the neighbors didn't know each other and had only said hello in passing. It was a wonderful time to meet each other. Lasting bonds were forged. And in it, it was an amazing time to share Jesus's love with each other. When asked what prompted us to do it, we were able to say that it was Jesus's idea, that He wanted us to get together and be friends. That party changed the face of the street. Neighbors began taking each other's garbage bins in, shoveling each other's drives and sidewalks, cutting each other's lawns. It became a face of "family" instead of strangers living side by side. He had orchestrated it, and it flourished into something bigger than we could have ever dreamed.

The following spring, we again asked in our little prayer circle what we could do, and this time, He instructed us to do a street garage sale—with many other details that would make it stand out. Ads were posted in the local newspapers, and balloons and signs were hung on the surrounding street posts leading onto our street. All neighbors participated drawing a huge crowd. We had planned a neighborhood barbeque at noon after the shoppers had left. But what we anticipated was nothing to what transpired. By 7:15 a.m., there were cars double parked up and down the street. Hundreds of people strolling the sidewalks. All neighbors who participated sold most of what they had put out, raising hundreds of dollars for each family. By noon, the crowds had died down, and under the shade of our front tree, we set up the barbeque and coolers. We provided all the hotdogs and hamburgers, and those who wanted to chip in to help pay for it offered, but we instead asked them to drop a donation into a jar for the local downtown youth mission. At 3:00 p.m. neighbors were still milling around, lounging on the curb, enjoying each other's company. It was a blissful day of building friendships, earning money, and raising funds for God's house. Something that seems so mundane—a garage sale—turned into another amazing time to shout God's glory to the world.

Eight months earlier, sitting on my front porch rocker, I had no idea what my obedience in asking those two women to pray with me would lead to. One single act of obedience in stepping out in something I was pretty scared to do led to the transformation of a street and the opening of heaven for God's glory over a neighborhood. Easy, simple. Just pray with two others. Get off of my porch, step out in faith that something will happen if I open my mouth, and watch what the Lord will do. And "do" He did!

The Foodie Faith Portal

I love to cook. I love to eat. I love to cook and watch others eat. There is nothing more satisfying when it comes to food than creating a masterpiece of goodness that makes others sit up with anticipation as they see it coming to the table. Having it melt in my mouth as my taste buds send feel-goods through my entire being. Mmm, food.

When I become pregnant with my second daughter, food no longer had the appeal it once did. By week seven of pregnancy, I was unable to keep anything in my belly. I had morning sickness each and every day. I was hungry. But unable to eat. On the first day of week thirteen, I woke up and thought, *"I am hungry."* And I made a dash to the kitchen and gobbled down breakfast. It wasn't until after I was finished that I realized that there was no morning sickness. No nausea. No vomiting. No shakes or waves of hot flashes. I felt fantastic! And I could eat! I made myself a big lunch, and for supper, I made one of my favorites: sweet and sour pork chops. With rice. And sauce. Lots of sauce. As my family and I sat down to eat dinner that evening, I almost was beside myself with anticipation of the yummy goodness I was about to take in. My taste buds squirted. It smelled so good. I cut a big piece of pork chop and placed it in my mouth. And before I could get it down my throat, I immediately projectile-vomited the remains of the day's worth of food across the table. My poor husband. He, too, was now done with dinner. I began to cry. I said, "God, I have a baby inside of me that I need to feed. I have to eat. I ate this morning and this afternoon, and I need to eat. I need to eat meat to properly feed her!" On and on I cried.

When I stopped crying and whining, I heard the small, still voice of my God say, "I want you to be vegetarian."

What? I said inside. *I cannot be a vegetarian. I have a baby to feed. This baby needs meat. I need meat to be healthy. We need meat.* On and on I argued with God, as if He didn't know what I needed.

When I stopped, He said again, "I want you to be vegetarian."

Hmm, I thought. *Well, if you want me to be vegetarian, then I will need a clear-cut sign from You that this really is Your voice I am hearing, because I don't understand how I am going to take care of my child and help her grow properly without meat.* With that, I went off to bed.

The next day at work, my Federal Express delivery driver came in. She is gorgeous and always looks fabulous. Her skin is amazing, wrinkle-free, and her body is in great shape. That particular day, we were chatting about our children, and she told me that her daughter was doing great in university that year. I was flabbergasted! What? She had a child old enough to be in university? I honestly thought she was in her middle to late twenties, not near old enough to have a child in university. I told her my thoughts, at which she laughed and said she was almost forty years old. Forty! I couldn't believe it. I told her how young I thought she was and how amazing she looked for her age. She then began to tell me how she was a vegan and hadn't ingested animal products in years and that was why her skin looked so great and she was so healthy. She said that she had something in her truck for me. She went out to her truck and came back with an entire folder full of information on becoming a vegetarian. She said she woke up that morning and knew she was going to meet someone that she should give the information to. It was me. I laughed and laughed and told her the story of my conversation with God the night before. She had a difficult time believing she had been a pawn in His plan for me to be a vegetarian, but she couldn't really argue it.

I then spent the next few weeks reading everything she had given me and going on every website I could find regarding being a healthy vegetarian. I discussed it with my midwife at my next prenatal appointment, and she, also being a vegetarian, knew the health benefits of being one. With her guidance and additional information regarding being a healthy and responsible veggie, I progressed through my pregnancy with flying colors. She insisted on monthly blood tests to ensure that my protein, iron, and vitamin levels were where they should be, to which the technicians stated that my protein levels were better than most carnivores'. My baby was born incredibly healthy, and to this day, she will choose a bowl full of beans over a plate of steak.

I don't know why the Lord wanted me to become a vegetarian. Was it to see if I would be obedient or not? He knew what the outcome would be, but I didn't. It was a big deal for me to give up eating animal products. I enjoyed eating meat. I loved milk. But if He asked me to, well, He knew best. And best is what I got! An exceptional pregnancy, a very healthy baby, a body that went back into shape within days of delivery, and a clear conscience that I am not contributing to animal torture for the sake of food. I learned how to eat healthy, how to consume certain foods together for the best absorption by my body, what foods are directly linked to re-actions and pain triggers in our bodies, and so on. Was it difficult? It could have been. But having full trust that my Creator and Dad in heaven knew what was best for me made it easy. I think having this obedience lesson under my belt has strengthened my faith for the next big test, and the one after that. If we can be obedient in the seemingly non-kingdom related items, then He can begin to trust us with more important matters. He knows when we are ready for big tests of faith, but we don't. We need to build our spiritual "muscles" and strengthen up. If we can lift ten pounds of being faithful, then we can lift fifteen. If we can lift fifteen pounds, then we are ready for twenty. He doesn't need to test our faith. He knows where we are at. *We* need the tests of faith to show ourselves how big our muscles are growing and have a faith memory to fall back on when the next lesson comes. Becoming a vegetarian was a lesson. A big part of me where I had little faith to believe that all would be fine if I let go and trusted. A lesson in trust and a lesson in faith. I passed.

Faith for Salvation

My dad's body died at the young age of seventy-two. His heart and will to live had died years earlier. I really only got to know him starting when he was seventy-one. He was there while I was growing up, and we had spent our lives together, but I didn't *know* him until it was too late to make a difference. I knew his outward self, but not much of his inward self. For the outside, extravagant but simple living well described him. That was my dad. Everything he did he did with passion. "Good enough" was never good enough. Every detail of something important had to be taken care of. Passion. I had learned many things from my dad, and most of those things I truly realized in the last few months, weeks, and days of his earthly life.

The day after he passed, my mom, my daughters, and I sat and looked at all of our family pictures, looking for the perfect ones that encapsulated who my dad was, ones that we could put on the slide show and the poster boards for his funeral. Pictures that perfectly embodied who he was, what he loved, and how he felt about life. There were so many to choose from. I learned a lot about my dad from the pictures.

There were hundreds and hundreds of pictures of cars that Dad worked on, restored, and resurrected. He was passionate about cars. They were living to him. He drew life from them. I'm not sure there was anything that Dad loved more than the satisfaction of finishing a car to perfect beauty. No dent was left unfixed. No ding went without notice. No scratch, nick, or speck of dirt was allowed. It didn't matter if the owner of the vehicle couldn't pay (or wouldn't pay); Dad would always finish the job. He did it for the *car*. Dad had a job he loved, and I am pretty sure that it never really seemed like work to him—it was his love.

I remember sitting for hours on end on his homemade metal

stool covered in paint and Bondo, watching him work. He would bang, weld, body fill, chisel, start again—everything had to be perfect. He communed with the car. He talked to it. He and the car would sing Dolly Parton, Loretta Lynn, and Johnny Cash songs for hours while he brought it back to life. He taught me to do my best at everything I put my hand to, no matter how menial a task—if you're going to do it, be passionate about it. And passionate he was.

I don't think I have enough fingers and toes to count how many folders of pictures I opened that were filled with pictures of ice storms and snowstorms. Hundreds and hundreds of pictures of them. Pictures of trees bent low under the weight they bore. Berries enrobed by little icy jewels. Shrubs and spring flowers frozen in a moment of time. Snowbanks built towering high above the roof of the car in the driveway, tunnels snow-blown through the backyard to the bird feeder two hundred feet beyond. What we saw as an inconvenience that day and a waste of film a few days later when the pictures were developed, Dad saw as beauty that he wanted to remember forever. Dad saw the raw power in it, and the raw power of the Creator behind it. Dad saw the magnificence of the scene that unfolded in front of him and honored the Magnificent One who created it. Dad relished the awesomeness of nature.

My dad loved airplanes and anything that had anything to do with flying. Again, folders and folders full of pictures of airshows. Dad couldn't get enough. And it didn't matter how many sky pictures we had of the Snowbirds; he would still take his camera faithfully to make sure he didn't miss a shot of them flying in formation. I don't know if there was anything specific that one could say was the reason he loved them—was it their power? Their magnificence of engineering? The thought that they carried us above the earth? Or was it that they exploded his imagination into the depths of the unmeasurable and impossible? I used to watch my dad's spirit soar from his perch on the ground. His eyes would dance with excitement, and his body would tense with every roar of afterburner. His passion for living and dreaming exploded when he was around aircraft.

Some would call my dad a dreamer. I call him an inventor. He taught us to dream, to imagine, and to try. There wasn't anything my dad wouldn't try to make. If he could dream it, he could make it. The pictures we found of things, bizarre things, that Dad made. But each had a purpose. Each was unique and filled a need in an incredibly efficient way. If he had had the resources to patent things, my goodness, he would have been famous, and rich. Dad could make anything. He was brilliant. We and everyone else around knew that if there was something that needing fixing, needed revamping, needed an end result but couldn't figure out how to get there, Dad could. We used to get so irritated by his storehouses of empty bleach bottles, Tide boxes, cardboard, and Styrofoam pellets. But the things he created when we needed something were unreal. Dad made hat and glove holders from two-liter pop bottles. He made horse tack keepers and bridle hangers from revamped bleach bottles. Carrying cases for hot food from cardboard and end pieces of rope. The most efficient air filter for when he painted in the garage out of furnace filters and an old fan. He taught us to dream, to imagine, and then to put it to paper. He would lead us step by step until we arrived at the same conclusion that he was at, and then would he help us bring it to fruition. His passion for trying was unsurpassed.

My dad loved to eat. He relished food. There was nothing more that Dad loved than his fried onion and ham omelets on toast. With cheese. And ketchup. Or maybe it was Mom's roast beef and mashed potatoes and gravy. Dad would plop on the butter, slop on the gravy, and douse everything in salt. He loved flavor. He loved eating. We used to get irritated because he would always take so long to eat, and would still be eating his meal even after we had finished dessert. I now see that it was because he was relishing his meal. We ate for sustenance. Dad ate for enjoyment. He was extravagant about food. He was passionate about eating.

In looking at the pictures, I learned so much about my dad that I had never realized before. He was driven to do the best he could. Whether it was fixing cars, cutting the grass, or growing ginormous sunflowers and zucchinis, Dad put his heart and soul into it. Dad's love language was gifts and acts of service. He was not eloquent with words, but he loved on us kids more than we will ever know. From every wrecked car he fixed for my brothers to every car he let me drive the beans out of to over three hundred thousand kilometers, he was there for us. He may not have always had the gentlest words, but his kindness and love poured through his doing. Dad loved life. From every rodent he fed at the back door, to every tree he tried to rescue and stake up after a windstorm, to every tear he shed when he hung up the phone after talking to his twin, Dad had passion.

A few months before my dad passed away, he was housebound.

He would spend his afternoons sitting in the garage with the door open, talking to any passerby who would stop for a chat. In the last few months, he was confined to his apartment and then, nearer the end, too tired to even venture outside, confined to his room. I would come home from work, rush around with my children, study for an upcoming exam, clean my house, do chores, and so on. I would go downstairs and sit with Dad for ten or fifteen minutes, and then calling children or the buzzer of the washer would pull me away. Dad always said, "Everyone is so busy, no time for nothing!" I now realize how true his statement was. We live our lives rushing from appointment to appointment, chore to chore, have-to to have-to, and never stop to realize what's truly important: relationships. In the end, when we have spent all our time, energy, and resources on the have-tos, we then fall into the should-haves. I should have spent the time with Dad when he was alive. I should have let him talk on and on about whatever was on his mind instead of getting frustrated with stories I'd heard a thousand times. I should have taken him to the car dealership when he wanted to go, instead of when my calendar said I was available, I should have. The should-haves can eat you alive. They steal your peace and rob your joy. The should-haves leave you feeling hopeless and desperate for another chance. The should-haves.

Pull Over

Religion has a way of pushing Jesus to the side and teaching that salvation comes from how well you can follow their prescribed traditions and regulations, backing it up as "true" by extorting the

Scriptures. My dad was an incredibly generous man. He offered to fix every traveling minister's vehicle for free. When his health allowed it, he was always volunteering to serve on building committees or help with gardening duties and maintenance chores at the Kingdom Hall or provincial assemblies. But Dad didn't, or couldn't, attend the Witness meetings on a regular basis. Whether it was his physical health or his hurting heart that kept him out, I will have to wait until heaven to find out, but Dad carried overwhelming guilt over not following religion's prescribed duties until the day he died. He repeated over and over to me during his last days that he hoped that all that he had done was "good enough" for Jehovah. That Jehovah would accept it even though he didn't go to the weekly meetings regularly or go door-to-door every month as all "good" Witnesses are instructed to. The religion that he had held so dear was now causing his heart to waver on the brink of terror as he stared down death's door. *Is the paradise really real? Are the rules of the religion truly what will open the door to eternal life? Or is my lack of doing my one-way ticket to hell?* These thoughts tortured my dad by the minute.

Intercession for him and his true salvation became my never-ending cry. Praying that he would meet the real Jesus and have peace before he passed. Praying that he would see that what Ryan and I had found was the real deal, and not false religion, as his brainwashed mind had convinced him. I was a madwoman for declaring the Scriptures out over my dad while he was sleeping. "God does not desire any to perish but all to attain everlasting life, and *you* have attained everlasting life. My God says that whatever I ask and do not doubt but believe in my heart, I shall have. I have asked Him that you will meet Him before you die, and I believe it to be true. You do know Jesus as your Lord and Savior, and all who call upon His name will be saved. Therefore, you are saved!" Over and over again I prayed.

Three weeks before he passed, as I was heading to work, the Holy Spirit said, "Pull over. I have something to say." Yes sir, signal on, stopped. "Your dad's salvation is secure. Although he will never speak it out and you will not see it in the natural, he is coming home." Wowie wow, the Rhema word of God confirming that prayers had been answered and a man broken in spirit had not been passed over or forgotten! Hallelujah! Heavenly peace washed over me at that moment with utter inexplicable joy.

Be Still

I was speaking with a friend who was suffering terribly from a depressed state. She is an amazing Christian woman, but sometimes the enemy sneaks up on her and within a few days she goes from not feeling great about herself to wanting to check out from this world. When she discusses this problem with friends or mentors, or reads books of advice, all have a formula for how to get out of the depressed state. Read this book, read these verses of the Bible in this order, pray this way, bind this, lose that, say this, and so on. And she simply stated, "I'm tired. I can barely get out of bed in the morning and put sweatpants on; how can I possibly formulate a plan and do all these other things if that is what I have to do to get out of this depression? I can't do it. I am tired of trying. There is no more that I can do that will stop this cycle of depression from coming like it does. I can't do it." And she is absolutely right. She cannot. Neither could I. But He can.

My entire upbringing as a Jehovah's Witness was about *doing*. Attend all the meetings, go door-to-door at least ten hours per month (sixty hours per month over summer holidays), answer a question at least once per meeting, come to the meetings with your books underlined and highlighted, wear skirts that come below your knee—this "do" list went on and on. If I did all these things and did them well, then God would love me. Then I was acceptable.

But then I met the real Jehovah and the real Jesus. I discovered that the Holy Spirit was not "God's active force, like electricity," as I had been taught by Jehovah's Witnesses, but instead the third Person of the Godhead who is tangible and real and here to teach me and comfort me and love me the way that Jesus the Son did with His disciples while He was earth. He showed me that there is nothing I can do to make Him love me any more than He does right now. There is nothing that any religion can tell me to do that makes me better or more acceptable to Him than I am right at this very moment. And there is nothing we can do in our own strengths that will heal the hurt in our hearts or the habitual cycles in our heads of depression or suicide thoughts—nothing in our own strength that will last.

Psalm 23 is a passage that everyone knows. Those who don't follow Jesus know it. It is read at every funeral and has found its way even onto T-shirts, with the verses twisted into slander. But do we really know it? Do we really believe that God wants us to just lie down? To just relax?

"Seriously? You don't want me to be involved in this ministry and that ministry and volunteer here and there? I can just be? It's okay to sit down in church, or even lie down on the floor when the one leading the service has just told me to stand or sit or kneel? It's okay to make a date with my Husband in heaven and just lie on the couch—not talking? Don't I have to pray? Don't I have to talk and converse or ask or *do something*? Don't I have to have my journal out and my Bible ready and ask Him to give me verses to read, and then read and read and wait for Him to speak to me that way?"

"He leads me beside still water. He makes me lie down in green pastures." Still waters and green pastures are not indicative of work. They are indicative of rest. "Be still and know that I am God" (Psalm 46:10). We see it on bumper stickers on cars that are racing to work. We see it on Bible cases that are carried to and fro, from this church to that meeting to this ministry. Do we really understand that it means exactly what it says? *Be still. Sit down. Take a load off. Relax.* This does not mean sit on the couch with a bag of chippies and watch movies for five hours before bed. That is the world's idea of relaxing. It means, *be still. Lie down in His presence, and ask Him to meet you. Then wait. Be still.* Stop talking. Stop asking. Stop thinking. Let the Lord of heaven refresh you from the water in the still waters.

Ryan and I have been together for fifteen years at the time of this writing and married for twelve. We each now know what the other is thinking. We finish each other's sentences and many times don't even need to start the sentences. We know each other so well that most times, words are not necessary. If it is in terms of endearment, we don't need words to convey our thoughts. We speak heart to heart. If it is in words of activities or looking for something or going somewhere, our hearts advise us before the words are even spoken. We could be out driving and nowhere near a Tim Horton's, but I will instantly know Ryan's thoughts and respond "yes" before he has a chance to even ask me if I want a tea. I know his heart. Our souls have become one, and in that, words in most instances are no longer required.

That is the place our Father God wants us to get with Him: where we are able to lie down, *be still,* and just *be* with Him. Words are not necessary. Where we can trust that He is capable of reading our hearts filled with love for Him and we don't have to tell Him with words. Where He can pour His love out on us and we don't have to use our ears to hear it. It just flows from heart to heart.

Most Christians know the beginning of Psalm 46:10: "Be still and know that I am God." We have that one memorized. But do we know the rest of it? "I will be exalted among the nations, I will be exalted among the earth!" That tells me if I am *still* and just *know* that He is God, then *He* will be exalted! Be still and watch Him be exalted in my life, and be exalted in all the earth!

I am by no means saying don't go to work or church or take care of your family, but I am speaking to the striving that we do in our lives to try to fix ourselves, to try to feel better about ourselves by being busy and involved. I know of many ministry leaders, pastors, international traveling evangelists, businessmen and women, who are ridiculously busy in their work, but in their work, they have learned how to rest and be still, to *trust* that He is in charge and step back and let Him be exalted through their being still. Jesus was busy, always moving, but in that, He mentioned over and over again that He "went away by Himself to the mountain to pray" (Matthew 14:23). We go to the "mountain" to hear the Father's voice, to see what is happening in heaven, to hear His direction, to feel His love, to take spiritual communion with Him. But to do these things, we must be still. We must be quiet. Our mountains may be our couches, it may be our exercise mats on the floor, and it may be our car on our radio-turned-off commutes to work. But it must be a decisive act to *be still, and let Him be exalted*. He has taught me to be still. And in that, He has been exalted in my life.

Being over Doing

My husband grew up in a predominantly Jamaican community in Mississauga. There is a saying there: "He's on Jamaican time." Meaning Jamaicans get there when they get there. They never arrive late; they arrive precisely when they intend to, which is— whenever they get there. Family and relationships are priority. They live simple lives, and they enjoy every day to the fullest. From what I have heard, life is not about accomplishments, but about *living*. Near the end of my dad's life, some incredible wisdom and proverbs came from his lips. He often said, "Much is said and done, but in the end, more will be said than done." "One's worries are sufficient for today; don't carry them into tomorrow." "Remember, your children, *are children*; let them *be* children." One that he said often is as noted above, "Everyone is so busy, no time for nothing." "No time for nothing" really meant no time for anything that really matters. I believe in the last few months of my dad's life, he realized that all the years and years that he spent working months at a time with no breaks were for nothing. As he sat there with nothing to do but contemplate his past, he realized a truth that he was desperate to pass on to us, his children: accomplishments and busyness mean nothing, and relationships mean everything.

How much time did I waste in the last few months of Dad's life cleaning, doing laundry, striving, running, *doing,* when really, the most important thing I could have been doing was just *being.* Being with my dad, holding his hand, listening to him, talking to him, loving him. I made excuses. I said, "I have to study because I have to get my licence to keep my job. I have to do laundry, I have to clean my house, I have to ..." The have-tos are as bad as the should-haves. Is this writing a case of the guilts? No. I have asked my Jesus to forgive me. There is no condemnation for those who are in Christ. I will not carry guilt. But I will learn my lesson. I won't make the same mistakes again. I won't put stuff ahead of people. I won't let my own anger, resentment, or desires come before those of the ones I love. I will enjoy every ounce of life I am given. I will appreciate every breath I take. And I will hear—and listen to—the wisdom of my dad. Wisdom listened to halfway through life is better than wisdom not listened to all at.

In the last few weeks and specifically the last few days of his life, I spent many hours with my dad, just him and I. I learned how much he loved. I learned how much he cared. I learned how much he hurt. I also learned how wise he was. I always knew it, but I was too busy to pay attention. Too busy with life. Too busy with the have-tos.

It was only on Sunday night, when I sat by his still, lifeless body that I realized he was right. That my time here with him was gone and that a great amount of time that I did have had been wasted because I was too busy with what really wasn't important. It was in that moment that Dad's epiphany hit home. I believe Dad made his realization about busyness in his last year. That you can work and toil and sweat and *do*, but in the end, all that matters are relationships and love. I believe he was trying to get me to understand what he had concluded, so that I was never to put *doing* ahead of *being*.

Sometimes when we remember someone, we remember what we saw last of the person. Broken bodies, broken minds, broken. We remember hurts and arguments and irritations. But despite my dad's broken body and a mind tortured by medications, there was nothing broken about his spirit. He knew who he was and whom he was loved by. His faith was strong in his religion, and his love burned strong for Mom, us kids, his grandchildren, and his brothers and sisters. He wept when he thought of those he hadn't seen in a while and rejoiced with such gladness after visitors came and spent time with him. Dad's eyes danced when Genevieve drew pictures for him and when Evangeline ran into his arms yelling, *"Papa!"* His body relaxed and his mouth softened into a smile when I sang hymns to him as he slept. He had an incredible capability for forgetting hurts and embracing the love when it was given. My dad's spirit man was nothing of broken.

When Dad went into the hospital, he began writing. He wrote on every scrap piece of paper and prescription he could find. He wrote about memories, names of friends long gone, cars he had fixed, and places he had been. He came home in time for Father's Day, and I wanted to make sure he got the perfect gift. I felt it was a journal. Then the search for the perfect one, which I found. Its nondescript beauty in the brown-on-brown leather mimicked my dad. The gold leaf was Dad too; he loved jewellery and embellishments. But it was the poem that captivated me and moved Dad to tears. The poem embodied Dad's life. The times when we didn't understand him, the times when he felt alone, the times when he was too tired to fight. The poem encompassed Dad's entire life to a tee. The poem was the famous "Footprints."

The journal pages now remain inkless. Within days of receiving the journal, Dad was too weak to write in it. But the pages are not blank. They are filled with memories of life and love and hurt and victories. They are filled with my dad.

The last night Dad was at home, I sat with him for three hours while he was in and out of fitful dreams and hallucinations. At one time, he sat bolt upright, crying, "Where's my body? Where's my body?"

I said, "Dad, you are in your body, in your chair."

He looked straight at me and said, "I saw Jesus. I saw Jesus holding out His hand to me, but I told Him I wasn't ready to go yet. I need to see your brothers." We called the ambulance shortly after that, and that was the last time he was home. A week after that, he was moved to palliative care, and we got the call to come; it was time. He was fitful again, having terrible nightmares, with his body convulsing. He wasn't awake or conscious in the present. I asked my Lord to let me talk to my dad in his spirit man. I closed my eyes, and I saw Dad to the left of me in a long tunnel, the tunnel of death. To the right, I saw Jesus. He was holding a door open, and there was such a bright light shining from behind Him that I couldn't even look that way straight on. I spoke to my dad in that moment in my spirit. He and I communed. I told him it was all right to go. He said he was scared. He couldn't leave my mom. I promised him I would look after her and that it was okay to go. He walked toward Jesus, I saw him move halfway. He then looked at me, spirit to spirit, and said he wasn't quite ready. I said that was okay; I was more than happy to have him a little while longer. I opened my physical eyes, and his body was calm. He slept peacefully and soundly for two hours. Mom and I left in the morning knowing we had a few more days with him. Each day when I went to see him, his body was more and more deteriorated, but his spirit was as strong as ever. My dad knew who his God was, and it was his faith that carried him. Even though he wasn't sure that what he had been taught all his life was true, and even though he wasn't really positive what happened after death, he knew his salvation was secure. His spirit man held tight to his God.

On my drive to the hospital after receiving the call from Mom that Dad was gone, the Holy Spirit clearly and audibly told me that Dad was in heaven with Jesus. He was in his new spirit-body, he was pain-free, and I would be with him when I got there. But I was allowed to see him with my spirit right then. I saw Dad, and he was beaming. He had the best smile on his face, a smile I didn't get to see too often when he was here. Through incredible sadness, I had immense peace. I know my Jesus is faithful. He said that whatever I ask and do not doubt in my heart, I will receive. I asked for my dad to be saved. Jesus says that he came to save all who were lost. He said that He does not desire any to perish but all to turn to repentance and be saved. And now my dad has the reward. I know Dad saw hell. He smelled it. He heard the cries of those who have gone there. I was there when he was crying out and screaming, *"No!"* It was just before he said he saw Jesus. I know my dad is in heaven. Thank you, Jesus, for all You are and all You have done. All glory and praise and honor be to the One who sits on the throne, and to the Lamb!

The intercessions for loved ones who have not met Jesus yet are by far the ones that wrench our hearts the most. They wrench our heavenly Father's too. I had seven years of knowing the real God in heaven before Dad passed away, and seven years of praying he would meet my Jesus and revel in His love before he left this earth. The "salvation for others" faith portal has to be the biggest one there is. But when we let go of our unbelief, it will become the biggest direct portal from heaven to us for faith to pass through. It will become the biggest reservoir in our entire being where faith can reside and grow.

Goodbye, Daddy, till we meet again.

Chapter 10

Mile Marker Two

We all have markers in our lifetimes that we can look back on and know that life, as we knew it, changed because of that event. It may be a geographical move, a marriage, or the death of a loved one. But each of us has those three or four large moments in life that change the direction of our lives forever. Sometimes life transitions and the lines between them are blurred from the before and after. The markers, the one-time "old ending and new beginning" times, only happen a few times throughout one's life, but the transformation that takes place is forever inscribed.

Growing up as a Jehovah's Witness blurred into a teenagerhood of not being accepted by my Witness peers as cool. That blurred into being accepted by my non-Witness coworkers as somewhat cool. That progressed to living a double life—still wanting to cling to what I had been taught was supposedly right and true and still going through the motions that religion demanded, but outside the confines of the religion moving into partying and craving being accepted by someone, anyone, who would let me into his or her circle. That cycled into bad relationships and bad behavior, which then blurred into my drifting away from the religion and the people in it, though not making a final stand for myself and cutting the ties. I continued the transition from one world to another, dating and partying and then meeting my Ryan, working, and existing. There was no clear cut "marker" that defined or altered the path of my life in those first twenty-nine years. Each year blurred into the year before, a gradual downward spiral of self-destruction. Then I met Jesus.

The day that we walked into YesChurch and for the first time met the Holy Spirit, my life began the halting of the trainwreck I was aboard. Weeping and sobbing uncontrollably three Sundays in a row and not knowing why was a large clue. I knew in my inner woman that something was about to change in my life. That if we continued to go to that church, my life was going to change forever. I didn't know how, though. I knew I didn't want religion again that demanded works and whitewashed sinful behavior, but I knew that this was different. This was real. Then I met Jesus. The day He walked into my living room, I was forever changed. He visited me, He forgave me, He washed me clean with His sacrificial blood, and my life was changed. That event in my life (I use the word *event* loosely here, for sake of story; it was sooo not just an *event*) was mile marker number one. The first clear, distinct marker that changed the direction of my life forever. The life that was headed for destruction and eternal hellfire was redeemed and turned around. Thank you, Lord!

In the next six years, many milestones were placed that paved the road of this new direction. Our marriage, the birth of two beautiful daughters, personal spiritual growth moving into church leadership, tons of miracles, two houses, new city, new church, and so many more. Each of these milestones was paved upon the last one laid, creating a patchwork of life threaded one through another. Milestones, not mile markers.

The second mile marker came October 2009. We had moved from our hometown of Brantford to Woodstock in May 2009. My dad's health was declining, and we made the decision to join our two homes and have Mom and Dad live with us. Our Lord provided the perfect brand-new house for us that allowed us to build an incredible apartment in the walk-out basement for my parents to live in. They would have their own space but would still be close enough that should they need anything, we would be upstairs for them. Ryan's work was now only three minutes away instead of forty, and we couldn't believe the grand favor we were living in. My husband had a wonderful job and there was no financial need for me to work. I stayed home with my girls, prayed with women in the church, went to weekly Bible studies, and was part of church weekly ministries. Once September came, we decided to home-school our children instead of sending them to public school. This was year six of living in this life path that Jesus had laid out for us, and things were going wonderfully, thus causing me to be completely blindsided when the second mile marker came that would again change the direction of my life.

Ryan came home on Monday night from work and was quiet. He didn't love on his girls as he normally did when he walked through the door. He sat at the table but didn't touch his dinner plate. Then the phone rang. We have strict policy in our home that we do not answer the phone during family mealtimes. But that night, Ryan chose to answer it. Not only did he answer it, but he also walked out to the front porch and closed the door behind him. Both of these two things were incredibly alarming to me. The phone rang with a local caller ring. There was no one in Woodstock that we had met yet that Ryan was on a friendly basis with who would call at dinnertime and require him to go outside to chat. My head was reeling! I could hear him whispering. Was he having an affair on me? TV drama flashed in my mind of thousands of scenes that looked just like this. Had he begun dating someone at work and needed to have privacy to speak to her? What was going on? He came back in and didn't say a word. After a few more moments, he excused himself and went upstairs to shower, stating that he wasn't hungry right at the moment. I was completely dumbfounded. But in my frustration with his silence, I heard the Holy Spirit say, "Leave him be and trust. Continue with your plans for the evening."

I was involved with the Healing Wells prayer ministry at our church in Stratford and had to leave within minutes of Ryan going upstairs. I chose to be obedient to the Holy Spirit's guidance, asked Ryan if he was okay, and then told him I was going and would be home at 11:00 p.m. As soon as I was out of the driveway and around the corner, I began to cry. Crying because I didn't know what was going on, crying in fear, crying. I had to make a conscious choice to pull myself together, as the evening was about others and not about me and my issues. Praying all the way there, interceding for those who would come for prayer and asking how Jesus would use me to help them, I momentarily got lost in Him and forgot about what awaited me at home. As I came to the homestretch of country roads before entering Stratford, I clearly heard my Jesus tell me to pull over. Yes, Sir—signal on, off to the side of the road. Daily in my walk with Jesus, He and I converse in the same manner that you speak to your friend or another person around you. Conversation about the daily doings of life. But there are a few moments that are clearly defined in my mind of His speaking to me words that are forever embedded in the framework of my memory. This was one of them. Gently but firmly He said, "Daughter, Ryan is not having an affair on you. However, hard times are coming. Know that you are in the palm of My hand, and I am your Provider."

What does that mean? My head was reeling. I had no idea. I replayed His voice over and over again in my mind on the final drive to church. I asked my Holy Spirit to keep my mind focused during ministry time, and on the way home, I prayed that He would direct me in handling what waited for me behind my front door. I had no idea or even an inkling of what was about to transpire.

As I entered our house, all was quiet. Ryan was sitting on the couch with the TV off. I sat on the sofa opposite him and asked him how his evening was. He didn't answer; he just looked at me. I then asked him what was wrong. After what seemed like an eternity, he choked out the words, "I lost my job." In that moment of time, my mind spun through the implications of what that statement meant. Our entire life was built around his job. We had just purchased a massive house and moved my parents in, promising to take care of them. We had two car payments and a large mortgage. My husband is one of the most amazing men I know, and to see him in that state of hurt and shame was the most painful thing I have ever had to go through. I wanted to take it from him. I wanted to fix it. But I couldn't. I could only sit there. In utter humility, he repeated over and over, "I'm sorry. I'm so sorry." And in that moment of time, nothing else mattered other than reassuring him that no matter what happened, my love for him wouldn't change. There was no anger; there was no fear. The Holy Spirit swooped in to remind me that Jesus had just told me that we were in the palm of His hand and that He was our Provider. I told Ryan that I already knew that this was coming. I told him what Jesus had told me hours earlier. In that moment of time, I knew this was a new mile marker in our life. I knew that from this moment on, our life would take a turn and not be the same as it was before.

Life did change as we knew it. Everything changed. We went doorbell ring to doorbell ring waiting for food and funds to show up to feed us and pay our bills. Ryan worked job to job for temp agencies for the next two years. I worked several temp jobs until I obtained my full-time insurance broker job eight months later. One of our cars got repossessed, and then we paid a ridiculous amount of money to get it back. Our children were enrolled in public school. My dad's health deteriorated exponentially from the stress of the situation we were in until he could bear it no longer, and he passed away. Everything in our natural life had changed. But in this brand-new direction the mile marker had turned us to, everything in the supernatural changed as well. We learned what it meant to really let God be our Provider. Our faith exploded exponentially under the pressure tests of fight or flight. Our children met Jesus and were changed forever. Our life experiences shared with others caused them to grow and change and draw closer to Jesus. What the devil had intended to use to destroy us made our marriage tighter and strengthened the threefold cord we have with our Maker so that it is now stronger than it ever was before.

I cannot tell you that if given the choice, I would want to go through it again. But I can tell you that I wouldn't change what I have learned or how I have grown for anything in the world. It is quite sad that it takes hard times to force us to draw near to our Creator. Life would be so much better if we drew near in the good and easy times. If we honestly took the time to draw near to Him in the good times, I am sure that there would be fewer bad times. And when the bad times came, they would be much easier to bear.

The following are e-mails that I had written to friends in the weeks and months that followed the emergence of mile marker two.

October 2009

Dear Friends,

It has been an interesting, humbling, exciting and tear-filled two weeks, yet tears not of sadness or despair, but of joy, awe, and the feeling of overwhelming love. In this new life chapter that began with the departing of Toyota from our life, we have seen our Great and Mighty God move His hand over our life to show what "Let Your kingdom come on earth" really means.

Many people say "God is my Provider," but until you are sitting at your kitchen table eating a casserole made from the last of the food in your fridge and not having a dime to buy anything else,

"God is my Provider" doesn't really mean anything. We had said those words over and over again, but until there is no paycheck and no more cash coming that you are aware of, the words aren't real. They have become real to us in this past two weeks. I write to tell all of you the awesomeness of our great God in heaven and how He truly does provide for His children, when we let Him.

We sat at our table two Mondays ago and ate the last of our "fridge food," with very, very little left in the pantry and nothing in the freezer. But God knew what we needed. Here is an account of the awesome miracle things that have happened in our lives in the past two weeks:

That Monday night, I had enough gas in the car to get to church for the healing ministry that I am involved in. While there, I felt in the pocket of my coat (which I did not take off that night) and I found forty dollars!

Also that night, while cooking, I had thought, *If I had celery and a bag of carrots, I could make some good soups and casseroles with the pantry grains we have left.* On Tuesday, Ryan took the forty dollars and bought a few perishable groceries that we needed, and that night at nine o'clock, a friend showed up at our door with *four boxes of food* for us, all things that we needed, including potty paper! Jesus used one of His daughters to get what we needed—His kingdom moving on earth!

The next day, someone we had only met a few times came to the door with more boxes of food and a cooler full of frozen food and meats! It was so overwhelming! Here is a wonderful woman who has seven children of her own and barely knows us, but knew our need and chose to share what she had, because she could, knowing that we needed it now and God would return it to her through someone else later.

Throughout last week, we had e-mail after e-mail from people we know and many more people we don't know but who had received an e-mail about our situation, e-mailing and offering prayer support and love.

Someone we have never met, who had received an e-mail from someone else we had never met, offering to take Ryan out to play golf for the morning, just to offer love and encouragement to him. Wow, this person has never even met us! But the Lord told him that Ryan needed some "man encouragement," and he stepped up to do that.

Later in the week, when I had no more gas and had to get Genevieve to her swimming lessons and gym time, I was given twenty dollars with no expectation of returning it.

We were given an empty Gold MasterCard and told to use it for whatever we needed it for.

Someone else I had only met once gave me fifty dollars.

Our homeschool group gave us seventy-five dollars in grocery cards (again, families that we hardly know).

Ryan got a great temp job for last Thursday and Friday where he had an opportunity to talk with the guy he was working with—that guy was in a "bad place," and God used Ryan to encourage him and pray with him.

Last Friday, someone else called whom we don't know but who had received an e-mail from someone else we don't know. This man was offering Ryan work for this past week, at a great hourly rate.

Last week, someone else from the homeschool group called and said that his work was hiring, and if Ryan brought a resume over, he would hand it in for him. That company called, and Ryan has an interview there this morning.

I was given a hundred dollars yesterday, again, and told to use it for what we needed, with no expectation of returning it.

The list goes on and on. I have been absolutely blown away by the love of our old friends and the love of people we have just met or haven't even met yet. We have now seen how "Let your kingdom come" really works. Sometimes we have had groceries left on our doorstep and have no human to thank for it, but this time it was different. I asked God, "Why didn't you just leave the groceries on the step like before?" but the answer I received showed me this time it was about heart issues, not about faith issues. It was about humbling ourselves to ask for help, pushing down the pride to accept the gifts that we know we cannot repay, and saying thank you over and over again. It also was about Him working through the ones He did and them being part of making "His kingdom come on earth."

One more miracle just right now! Ryan got home last night from his week-long job in Kingston and was told that he may or may not be paid today. Our mortgage comes due today, and we needed the money today. His boss called this morning and said that his paycheck is ready now to pick up! Another answer to prayer, God making sure that we are taken care of.

The lessons we have learned in the past few weeks are more than I can write. We have learned that when the money runs out and the job is cut off, we can either go into desperation and grief, or we can believe that the God we claim to belong to is real and cares about us and the Bible we preach really does apply to us right now. We chose door number two. And Jesus has proven Himself faithful. I am in awe of His grace on us, His love for us, and His faithfulness in keeping His word as written in the Bible, that He does take care of His people and His children will never beg for bread.

Anyway, I just wanted to let you all know what has been happening, and thank each and every one of you for your love, your phone calls, your prayers, your physical gifts and provisions. We have never felt so loved or cared for. This attempted blow by the devil to our lives has truly turned to such good! The initial hurt and shock of it all was all worth it for the love that we have gotten to feel from our friends and family. Thank you all!

December 2009

Hello, everyone. It has been five weeks since I wrote our last update on our life situation since this new chapter has started. First, I want to say thank you to all of you who have been praying for us. Your prayers have not gone unheard. Our God is so faithful and has taken such incredible care of us! My last e-mail update told of the first three weeks' worth of miraculous provisions and how our Lord had taken care of us. My e-mail ended with Ryan's one-week job calling and saying that he could come and pick up his paycheck, that they would get it ready for him on that Friday, even though they were not planning on doing it until the following Monday. He had also gotten a call for an interview from an employer whom he was directed to by one of our homeschool dads. Well, here is the rest of the story since that day.

Ryan got that job and started the following Monday

When we went to get his paycheck, it was *three hundred dollars* more than we were expecting, which paid another bill that was due the following week

We went to the bank, deposited the check for our mortgage withdrawal that day, and then called the bank to ask if they would withdraw the one-week deposit hold from the check (our bank holds checks for a week). After a half hour on the phone and an operator who was adamant in teaching me a lesson that they do not let checks pass, my God intervened as He had said He would, and the operator said fine, they would let the check go so that our mortgage wouldn't bounce! Thank you, Lord!

That day, we received a gift of a hundred dollars.

The next day, another mom from the homeschool group came to our home with an envelope from someone else who wanted to remain anonymous. It had five hundred dollars in it!

Ryan's new job is construction, and was told he would be traveling each week. This is his fifth week, and he has only been gone long distance two weeks total, with the rest of the time being local jobs! Thank you, Lord, for orchestrating it so that Ryan could be home with us!

For this job, Ryan needed winter construction clothes, boots, gloves, and so on before he could work. He was given four hundred dollars so he could buy those things and take this job!

Here's some fun stuff, just coolio things to let us know that Daddy cares about our wants and not just necessaries too. I had in the past at different times thought to myself, "I would like a pearl necklace—fake, of course!—a new vegan cookbook, new dress pants, and new jeans." (I wasn't asking Him for them; it was just random thoughts of "Ooo, I would like …") Daddy used His children to bring me each of these, out of the blue, randomly, just because! The best cookbook I have to date! Both pairs of pants fit perfectly! And the necklace is exactly the length and style I wanted! (PS, I never voiced any of these desires to anyone!)

Back to necessaries: I was given money for gas in my car.

Ryan was given twenty dollars with instructions to spend it on himself, for coffee breaks specifically on the job site.

We continue to have bags of milk, eggs, and desserts show up in our kitchen.

We were given an entire big Rubbermaid tub full of snacks!

Given another sixty dollars for groceries and a big box of staples and snacks.

Given another sixty dollars.

Given a one-hundred-dollar gift card, farm fresh eggs, and beautiful clothes for my girls.

Given two backpacks and bags full of winter clothes for my girls, including a snowsuit that Genevieve needed. It fit her perfectly!

Given another twenty dollars and a cooler full of meat and frozen food.

Given a forty-five-dollar gift card for a restaurant (thank you Daddy for another would-like-to-have, not just necessaries).

Given three hundred dollars.

Thank you to each and every one of you who had a part in the above. It has meant so much to us. As I write this, it sounds like we have just been spoiled rotten, and you know, we have been. But you never really know how much it takes to run a household, pay bills, and buy groceries until you don't have the money you used to have. It has been an incredible test of faith to believe the Bible when it says, "I have not seen the righteous forsaken, nor his descendants begging bread" (Psalm 37:25). We haven't had any extra, but thanks to each of these gifts, we have not missed or bounced any bills, other than the Infiniti payment. Thank you, our friends; we are so grateful to each of you.

Much good has come from this, including some huge lessons. About three weeks ago, I was beginning to internally whine about how the food was dwindling and no more was coming forth and I didn't have a job yet and Ryan's job wasn't enough, yadda yadda yadda. I was getting a little bitter because I knew that people were putting away money for RRSPs, their personal savings, etc. while we were suffering (I use that term loosely; I was on the pity-bus). Whine, whine, whine, poor me, poor me ... Then I heard the Holy Spirit's quiet, gentle voice say, "You are reaping what you sowed." He then gently reminded me of the many times when He has asked us to give money here to that person or that person, to give an offering to a traveling minister that we had gone to see, etc., and we bowed out, saying we couldn't afford it or we didn't have any extra money. God then pointed out in the driveway and showed me that we had hundreds and hundreds of dollars sitting out there in monthly payments.

I said, "God, we needed cars."

He said, "If you didn't have those payments, you could have

taken care of others when I asked you to." Does that mean we are not allowed to have nice cars? No, it just meant that we were reaping what we sowed. We chose to take care of our desires and fill our every want with little regard to others beyond our basic tithe, and that was largely what was being reaped as well. It has been a real eye-opener as to what money should really be for. Ryan had a really great job with a really great income, but we were fairly selfish with it. What a huge lesson in being generous. What goes around comes around. We will never know what tomorrow will bring, but if we plant the proper seeds today, we will reap the benefits tomorrow—in every aspect of life. God makes sure our needs are met, but when He takes care of us, He always makes sure He gives us enough to take care of others too. We "went to the penalty box for two minutes, and we felt shame." Repent, ask for forgiveness, and move on. The next day, food was coming again. Aghhh, we have to learn the life lessons! The exciting thing is, when we give away, He gives us back even more of what we could ever even think or imagine we wanted!

Another "lesson from the pity-bus" that I have learned: during my whining about being uncomfortable, I have been asked by the Lord, "Where do you live? Do you have food? Do you have cars? Do you have clothes? Do you have choices?" and so on, at which point I of course answer yes, and He reminds me to pray for the millions of others who do not have warm homes, choices in clothes or food, cars to drive, or indoor plumbing, for that matter. Needless to say, the bell rang immediately, and I got off the pity-bus.

We are very grateful for Ryan's job; it pays the mortgage. But right now, it pays nothing else. Yesterday morning, I was praying, and I said, "God, thank you for providing for our mortgage. Thank you for your children who have brought us food and grocery cards. Thank you. But where are we going to get the money to pay our bills? The phone/Internet/satellite will be cut off in five days, and it is two months' worth of use."

He asked me, "Haven't I provided for your mortgage?" I said yes. "Haven't I provided for your food?" I said yes. He said, "Don't you think I can provide for your bills too?" I had to say yes. Last night, we were given the amount we needed plus twenty dollars. We hadn't told anyone what we needed, but He did. And they listened. And our bill is paid. Thank you, Lord, for your obedient children who listened to you. (PS, I know that satellite and Internet are not normally necessities, but the satellite is to my parents, and the Internet is to find a job—thought I would throw that in.)

Many reading this may think we are taking advantage of friends, sponging off them, whatever. And you know, if this had happened to anyone else and I was the one reading these e-mails, I would be inclined to think the same thing. But that is not it at all. We spend hours a day sending out resumes, calling companies, and looking for jobs. Why nothing more is coming forth, I am sure there are reasons; I just don't know them yet. But I know one thing: through this, God is not only teaching us to trust Him for *everything* and to praise Him whether life is good or uncomfortable, but He is also teaching His other children how to be pawns in the kingdom, to make His kingdom come to earth by taking care of others.

I have not enjoyed this phase of my life very much. It is uncomfortable, and it is frustrating, but boy oh boy, have I learned a lot about me, about us: how selfish I have been, how uncaring I have been, how arrogant we have been in thinking that nothing will happen—and you know, I only write this so that each and every one of you can learn from our mistakes. Don't make the same ones and have to go through the same mess. Never take your jobs for granted, or the great or not-so-great paychecks you receive. Take care of your family, and then think of whom you can help before spending the rest on yourself. I know many of you already know that and are taking care of others, and we thank you so much! We have had such bad attitudes in the past. Thinking, "Well, God gave us this great job, and it is our money to spend any way we want; if they want more money, then they should work harder," blah blah blah ... We judged others and reasoned out why we shouldn't give them money even though we knew they needed it, thinking, "Well, if they wouldn't smoke or drink or whatever, then they would have money for food," and so on. Bottom line— what people do with their money is their business and between them and God, but what I do with my money is between me and God, and if He says that I need to be passing around the wealth that He has blessed us with, then I need to start obeying. The biblical principle of sowing and reaping applies whether we are Christians or not.

Our dear friends, we love you all so much and thank you again for all your financial, emotional, and prayer support. You never know what your mind will do until this kind of situation hits you, and to many on the outside, it's just a job loss. But to us, it has been our entire life turning upside down. Our entire way of living halted. Going to a quarter of your income is a very difficult transition to make when you are thrown into it with no warning. But each of you has made it so much easier, and we will be eternally grateful to you all. Your love has helped us keep our bellies full, our home intact, our sanity safe, and our faith strong. As I send this out, I pray that my God, my faithful Lord Jesus, will bless each of you a hundredfold for what you have sown into us. We love you.

February 2010

This is my prayer in the desert
when all that's within me feels dry;
this is my prayer in my hunger and need:
My God is the God who provides!

Well, it has been such a ride since our last update on our new life! Our incredible God has reigned in our hearts and our lives, and living under His provision and protective umbrella has been so much better than anything we ever had before! Thank you again, each of you dear friends, for your prayers and support. I know they are a great part of the reason we are so uplifted each day and able to face the mornings.

God has proven Himself supreme in our lives over and over again in the past few weeks, and I am just so in love with Him! Not because of what He has given, but because of the relationship that has grown with Him and getting to know Him so much better in the past while. It is too bad that trials in life turn us closer to God and that when we are in the "good times," sometimes we spend less time with Him. That has changed for me now. Here is another list of how God has physically provided for us. I write this not to brag, but to encourage you that He is our Provider and He absolutely sees and knows exactly what we need at all times.

We had *no* money for Christmas, obviously—but when I went to the employment center for interview training, I was given an invitation for "below poverty line families" to go and shop for gifts for their children at a local church. I was able to get each of my girls awesome, brand-new gifts, three each, for a total of eight dollars! Thank you, Lord, for your provision! Genevieve, she's a smart one; she knew we had no money for presents, but when she got up and saw them, she learned another lesson that her Jesus cares about what she wants, and not just what she needs!

The day before Christmas, we received a gift card for groceries, one for gas, and another for a restaurant from someone we don't even know! He had received my e-mails forwarded by someone else and wanted to bless us! *Thank you!* It meant so much to us, and it also meant we could buy groceries for another two weeks, and Ryan and I could go out on a date! Jesus knows what we need to keep going!

Another wonderful friend continues to keep us supplied with pantry goods like soup and cereal. Thank you, friend—it means so much to us!

We had a six-hundred-dollar random deposit into our account from the government —they had reviewed our income tax and decided they owed us more money! This coming the morning that our hot water and gas were going to be cut off and the Primus was going to be repossessed. We had enough to pay the bills and get groceries, again!

I opened a beautiful card last night, and in it were two more gift cards, one for groceries—Ryan was very excited because he got some *meat*!—and the other for recreation for us! Thank you again my friend, for your thoughtfulness!

> This is my prayer in the battle
> when triumph is still on its way:
> I am a conqueror and co-heir with Christ,
> and firm on His promise I'll stand!

Again, I write to let you know that *He will provide* for us, if we trust *Him* and not ourselves or the world's system, i.e. credit! Ooh, I wish I could cut open my heart so you could see how in love with my God I am. I am sooo glad that this trial has happened because of the good that has come out of it, the lessons that we have learned! When we stand on the promises that He has laid out in His Word, and we act in faith along with those promises, speaking out the truth of the promises and not the visual reality of what we see, then He can move on our behalf!

> I will bring praise!
> I will bring praise!
> No weapon formed against me shall remain.
> I will rejoice!
> I will declare

God is my victory,
and He is here!

I learned a vital lesson the past few weeks in regard to praise and prayer. I think most of us spend the majority of time in prayer reminding God of what we need, asking for blessings for our-selves, thinking that maybe He has forgotten about our daily needs. He reminded me that I don't need to do that anymore if I trust His Word in Matthew 6:33. Two weeks before the collection calls started coming for the gas, Primus and hot water tank, my Holy Spirit and I were having a chat, and He reminded me that Father God provided for our phone bill last month, and that I didn't have to ask for money anymore for our bills. He knows what we need, when we need it. That I should instead spend my prayer time in praise, worship, and intercession for others. So I listened. Then when the collections bills started coming, I ignored them, and I ignored the drive of my soul that was screaming out to ask for money. Instead, I spent that time in intercession. It came as no surprise on the day that the bills were to be cut off that we had the deposit of funds from the government. Thank you, Lord. What a huge lesson in *trusting* the Word, one hundred percent. No wavering or lukewarmness, and He takes care of us. Ooh, the Scriptures that speak of this, if we would only listen! "Do not be a man tossed to and fro," "Ask, and when you ask, believe that you have already received it," "Be hot or cold, but not lukewarm, for fear that you will be spat out," "Seek first His kingdom, and all other things will be added to you!" Thank you, Lord, for your faithfulness! Although we have had our moments of pity-busing, they are fewer and much further between. We have *chosen* to bring continuous praise to our God, not allowing this "weapon" that had been formed against us to prevail, and our God has been our victory!

> All of my life,
> in every season,
> *You are still God!*
> I have a reason to sing;
> I have a reason to worship.

We have learned that there is never a time not to sing or to worship, no matter what the season of life. It is so easy to praise when life is good, but when the trials come, do we cave and no longer praise, or continue on believing that our God really is real and cares about us? Sometimes it is so hard to sing or praise, but pushing through my soulful tendencies to sulk and making my lips move builds my spirit woman until she once again rules over my soul!

> This is my prayer in the harvest
> when favor and providence flow.
> I know I'm filled to be emptied again;
> this seed I've received I will sow.

The opportunities to wallow in our financial situations have been many these past few months—and I am not going to deceive you; I have had my moments. But most times, I have asked and *allowed* my Holy Spirit to strengthen me to press on toward the goal of doing my part for the kingdom coming to earth, and He has been faithful to keep me. Ryan and I continue to remember our job as preachers at all times, being ministers of the gospel everywhere we go, continuing to fulfil our commitments that we have made in ministries, and so on. From that Ryan has received incredible favor at his job. Not only does he have an entire "battlefield" to preach to, where he has had many, many opportunities to share Jesus with his coworkers and bring light into their darkness, but he has also received favor with his boss. When hired, he was told that he would be traveling most of the time—but I thank my Jesus every day that although Ryan has worked for this company for ten weeks now, he has traveled for only two! He has been fifteen minutes from home for the other eight weeks now! Thank you, Jesus! As well, he has been assigned coveted jobs at the worksite, easing the pressure on his back. Again, all praise and glory and honor be to Him who sits on the throne, and to the Lamb!

I continue to look for work. I have had a few interviews, but nothing has come to fruition as of yet. Many promises, but nothing solid. I will continue to spend hours applying, and I have asked my God to close every door that is not of Him and only to give me the job that He has assigned for me. Funny enough, I have no distress over not receiving the other jobs. I know the one He has for me will come, and until it does, He will continue to provide for us. I will continue to do my job of intercession and praise and worship, along with job hunting, and I have incredible peace to leave the rest with Him.

Thank you again to each of you for your love and support, and please continue on praying for us, if you will. The moments of temptation to cave in and give up come with great force, especially at times when we are tired. Pray for strength, that we will not give in under the pressure of the enemy, and that the above song will continue to be our anthem until we triumph in this battle! Ryan called just now to say that there is a rumour that layoffs are coming; pray that God's will be done in his life as far as work is concerned. If this is the job for him, pray that it will remain, but if God is moving Him on, pray that Ryan will have peace and contentment with that.

I love you all and pray that my amazing wonderful God would continue to sustain you and hold you until the day of His imminent coming!

PS. The song is "Desert Song" by Hillsong United—my new favorite!

There is so much now that I look back on as to who I was and what my thought patterns were before mile marker two. I see now that if mile marker two hadn't happened and life had carried on as it was going, I would still be at the same spiritual level I was at before. I would still be on top of the world because of the natural circumstances that coddled me. Although I had spoken it, in the deep recesses of my mind, Jesus wasn't really my Provider or Keeper. Toyota was. But until put to the test, I didn't really understand it. I didn't understand how much we relied on Ryan's paycheck. How much our egos and pride were dependent on the five thousand dollars a month that he brought home. But now I know. We realized how big our egos were and how small our faith was. Although we had been told over and over again how much God had "fast-tracked" us in our faith from the time of becoming born-again, we realized that we had huge faith for the supernatural and miraculous to take place, but in the reality of day-to-day living, we really relied upon ourselves and our own self-sufficiency because we didn't need to rely on God to take care of our physical needs. Toyota did that for us. Our Lord had to strip away all that we held ourselves to and all that we trusted in to teach us how to really trust only Him. In all that we have gone through, there is nothing now that I will be unable to trust my Jesus in. He never let us down. His hand was always outstretched for us to take hold of. In fact, He never pulled it away. We did. His was always there.

This mile marker moved me from "faith in my faith" to true faith in Jesus. Yes, you read that correctly. I now have learned that I had "faith in my faith." I went from being a stay-at-home mom, homemaker, and full-time intercessor to working full-time in a town forty minutes away. The two to three hours per day that I used to spend in study, worship, and intercession are now condensed into my forty-minute drive, if I can stay alert enough to not drift off into commuter eyes (the glazed, deer-in-the-headlights look, a telltale sign of someone who has driven the same country roads for way too long and knows every turn and stone on the road like the back of her hand). Prior to mile marker two, somewhere along the way, the lines began to blur the difference between faith in my Lord and faith in my works. I felt that that the more I studied, prayed, and interceded for others, the more the Lord would bless me and use me. The more time I gave, the more powerful for Him I would be. My faith for miracles and supernatural occurrences hinged on how much time I spent in these things. How could I possibly go to Healing Wells and pray for healing if I hadn't spent two hours before the meeting in worship and prayer? What happened there was contingent on what I did before. Or so I thought. On this side of mile marker two, I was quickly and painfully taught the hidden error of my thinking. Now being down to little to no time to read my Bible and dissect it in study, a tired commute for intercession, and a drowsy passing out while saying bed time thank you's led me to listen to the lies of the enemy. He would whisper, "You are no good. You suck. Who do you think you are that you think you should still be interceding for others? You spend no time with your God and you think He will still bless you with words of knowledge and healing hands for others? You are mistaken. You must spend hours with Him before He will give you those gifts. You cannot do it anymore. You are not allowed anymore because you don't give enough to Him first."

I fell into deep sadness over what I had lost. I stopped offering to pray for others. Stopped asking injured people if they wanted Jesus to heal them. Stopped praying for my children when they got sick and offered them medicine instead. I thought the miracles that had happened when I prayed for people before were because of what I had accomplished. In my conscious mind, I never thought that, but it became clear that deep in the subconscious, this is what I really believed. That somehow, God must have been using me in those miraculous ways because I spent more time with Him than others. That He had given me those healing and prayer gifts as a payment for my offerings of time. And now I could not make that offering, so the gifts must have been lifted. But then once again, gentle and kind, my Holy Spirit would come and comfort me. He would ask me to pray for someone. I would say I couldn't. I hadn't spent any time in the past few days praying, so how could I pray for someone else? The power of the Lord couldn't possibly be on me anymore. But as He persisted and I opened my mouth to prove Him wrong (I know, twisted thinking that we do on the inside of our minds!), the power and anointing that used to come after hours of worship would be there instantly. He showed me it wasn't about me, and what works I had done were not what brought the power of heaven down. It was my obedience and willingness to open my mouth when requested. The power was always there. It was the faith *in Him* that activated it to bring about change in the natural world in front of me.

As time has moved on from the emerging of mile marker two in my life, he has taught me to have my spiritual antennae up at all times. I know when the Holy Spirit is getting my attention. I know what He *feels* like. I have learned to hear His voice in the midst of a crowd and pay attention when He calls my name. He has fine-tuned me and cemented the fact that the Father's love for me and use for me on earth are *not* contingent on my works, but on my willingness and obedience.

Mile markers sometimes are instantly wonderful, as was my first marker of meeting Jesus and having my life forever changed for the better. That mile marker came wrapped in the most beautiful gift wrap paper. The inside present waiting to be unwrapped was magnificent from the start, and I embraced it as a child does a brand-new toy on Christmas morning. But mile marker two was not so pleasantly gift-wrapped. It came in a torn brown paper bag and had a tough outer shell, requiring patience and tools to crack it open before the present was revealed. Once cracked, the inner core of the shell was not attractive. But the fruits of that inner core, accepted and worked at, have brought even greater change, peace, and joy than ever could have been anticipated by a shiny silver wrapper. What are your mile markers?

Chapter 11

My New Normal

I met Jesus when I was pregnant with my first child. After her birth, I took maternity leave for a year. At the end of the year, our financial situation was such that I didn't need to go back to work full-time, and I only worked two days per week. During the pregnancy in my first year of being born-again, I was at every meeting, every Bible study group, every church service I could attend. After her birth, I spent hours in the Word, studying, praying, devouring what my God was teaching me. When I did go back to work, it was not to my full-time career but instead to our church as a clerk, which still allowed me to be immersed in His presence and glory at all times. I remember vowing that I would never work in the secular field again. That work in God's house was way better, and I wouldn't waste the talents He gave me on something that wasn't building His kingdom.

Three years later, child number two was born. Again, I didn't need to go to work full-time and continued my stay-at-home mom/work part-time role. I had random part-time jobs here and there, but for the most part, each and every day included at least two to three hours in my prayer closet, at my study desk, at a meeting, or in a study group. And my Jesus met me. He would meet me in my room. We would talk for hours on end. The Holy Spirit would teach me and guide me as I studied the Word. He would explain things to me that I couldn't understand. It was Him and me. I loved it.

God began to mold my supernatural talents. He downloaded prophetic words and visions on a regular basis. He gave me words of knowledge. I would hear His voice in my head as voices outside my head were speaking, telling me what to say back to them. I saw supernatural visions more during my waking hours than I saw the natural realm with my physical eyes. He told me what people were going to say before they said it. He let me read their minds so I could speak their thoughts before they did, for the purpose of them instantly trusting that I was His servant and so they could believe that what I was going to speak was from Him. He fast-forwarded my learning curve and gave me intense understanding of His Words and ways. Worship, corporate and private, was intense. Visions, sightings of angels, prophetic words—all came fast and furious. I was convinced that He had given me these gifts and talents because I spent so much time with Him. I thought, *I spend time with You, and then You love me more and give me more stuff.* My understanding of His love became transactional. I began to believe that others didn't have what I had because they didn't spend the time with Him that I did. *I couldn't have been more wrong.*

When the time came that I needed to go back to work fulltime, I was pumped. I had had five years of being able to stay home and be with Him for extended lengths of time each day. My forty-minute commute time was me and Him. My lunch hour was me and Him. My commute home was me and Him. I was involved in two very intense para-church ministries that strengthened and stretched my faith. But as the months passed and months moved into a year and then two, my heart grew faint. Financial trials, the death of my dad, and the heartache of missing my girls became overwhelming. I got to the point where my mouth was too tired to formulate the words necessary to praise Him. My happy brain grew cloudy, and my energy to embrace change was sapped. But it was only when this happened that He could teach me that *He* is God, His love is not transactional, and He still loves me whether I am in "the closet" four hours a day or four minutes.

A New Smattitude

We attended a neighboring church, as one of our favorite worship leaders was going to be there that Sunday. Little did I know who would else would be there or the life-changing events that would transpire from it. As worship ended, an incredible woman and renowned author was introduced. I had seen her books at the bookstore but hadn't yet picked one up. As she began to tell her story, I was undone. Tears streamed down my face the entire time she spoke. Her life was forever changed by a one-time criminal act of her son. She spoke of the unthinkable life events that had unfolded for her family, events that no mother would ever dream she would have to go through. But in the face of the unbelievable, she stood to encourage others. I realized that even though my life circumstances couldn't ever compare to what her family had gone through, my situation might be difficult and I too could learn the life lessons that she had learned.

This beautiful woman talked about her life before the incarceration of her son. Her ideas, hopes and dreams. Then one event changed those ideals forever. She spoke of how she had a choice: either give up and die, or accept the "new normal" and move on, finding joy in the pain and paving new dreams and hopes. I sat there crying tears that I thought were compassion for her situation; I later realized they were tears shed for my "normal," which at this time seemed lost forever too.

My old normal was what I had always dreamed of: an amazing husband who had a wonderful job that allowed me to stay at home, homeschool my children, be with my parents, volunteer in local ministries, and spend hours a day in Bible study and worship. I had two small children whom I absolutely adored, and being with them every day was all I ever wanted. My husband obtained a transfer, which cut out his commute and allowed him to be home with us for four more hours every day. Then one day, he came home sad. Six hours later, he told me that his job was no more. Within five months, I was back to work full-time and commuting. My husband worked for temp agencies for two years, and financially "just getting by" became our new normal. We both worked very diligently at our jobs to do the best that we could and honor our God in all that we put our hands to. I began schooling for my vocational certification and had pursued excellence in my current position. It was not my dream to advance in the secular world, but living in my motto of, "If I have to do it, I will do my best at it," I worked diligently. Shifting two and half years forward, sitting in that church listening to this woman, I realized that I had been inwardly hoping for my old normal to return. Did I really want to be a businesswoman? No. Did I really want an upper management position in an office? No. Did I really want to travel the province doing sales training? No. I wanted to be home with my children, teaching them, playing with them, and nurturing them into all they could be. I wept that Sunday as I realized that "normal" might never be normal again. And I wept because as she spoke, I had a choice to make: either remain in the bitterness of not having my "life" that I missed, or accept my new normal and honestly give my one hundred percent to it. Then and only then could God fully utilize me in this new arena and move me into the future He had planned for me.

Devouring her newest book, I allowed God's encouragement and strength to come through her words and set out the following day with a new mindset. I would embrace my new normal. I would not cry and feel sorry for myself all the way to work and then begrudgingly trudge through the day. I would not collapse on the couch at night bitter that I had no energy left to play with my children. As she laid down her hopes and dreams on God's altar and determined in her heart to continue living—and thriving—in her new normal, I too did the same. *Okay, Lord. If I cannot homeschool my children and be a stay-at-home mom, I accept that. I will lay down my dreams of that life and thoroughly embrace this one. I will let go of the resentment and loss that I feel, and I will move into this new phase in my life with open arms.* As I drove to work that Monday morning, laying down all I had ever wanted on His altar, something broke in my spirit. That day, work was no longer a chore. I had a renewed vigor to accomplish my daily tasks. But something broke in the heavens as well. New business sales calls came flooding in. Good business that every salesperson dreams of getting on a regular basis was at my fingertips. Referrals from current clients. New phone-in business that had good history and was easy to sell and process. So much new business that I had to work extra hours just to keep up with it all and maintain my regular customer service workflow requirements. Do I dream of retiring from this corporation with a large pension and benefits? Do I dream of upper management and a six-figure-a-year salary? No. I still dream of being at home with my children while they are young and then becoming a missionary and evangelist. But do I hold bitterness in my heart that I cannot have that now? No. I have laid that down on the Lord's altar of human dreams, and I give my all to Him right now. I will continue to steal away the time that I can for Bible study and worship. I will cherish the few hours a day I have with my girls. I will take every opportunity to unofficially volunteer where I can. But I have determined in my heart that I will no longer allow the devil to steal the opportunities that I have *today* to enjoy this life that my God has given me. I will not give in to self-pity or bitterness. I will thrive in my new normal and be thankful every day for the life I do have. I have a new smattitude—that is a s'mover with a good attitude. S'mover? Someone who smiles and moves with purpose (www.givemore.com)!

Thank you, Lord, for giving your daughter the courage to bravely share her story with the world. Thank you, Lord, that you positioned me in that church that morning to hear it.

Chapter 12

Just Get Out of the Way

As the congregation worshipped, and as I had sensed in the past, there was a longing in the people to feel God's tangible presence, to hear His tangible voice, to see a vision of Him with open physical eyes. There is a longing to believe for those things but an unseen hidden force that tells them that it is not possible, that what they have is all there is, that it is wrong to long for those things, as they are not from God. That you shouldn't need those physical manifestations to worship God. That this is what our church services look like, and do not stray from it, as you will be a distraction to others. You will stand out. Others will stare. The viewers online will see you being different, and that will show disunity in the body if you don't conform to this box of how things are done here.

There is an unheard heart's cry that begs to scream out, "Jesus, come to me! Jesus, I want to see you! Jesus, I want more of you! Not more of your blessings, but just you!" But the realms of church protocol keep the people in their neat clothing and neat rows and neat worship of clapping on cue and jumping when told and shouting in response to the leading of the worship team—only when allowed and invited.

I looked up and saw a ceiling that was very low, mere feet above the heads of the church body. The ceiling was made up of the word *fear.* The letters were attached like cursive writing but block letters, and they covered the entire sanctuary. Fear is what causes the inhibitions of the worshippers from letting go. Fear is what drives the tithing sermons. Fear is what causes the people to be herded like cattle through the rituals of the morning, from the standing to the visiting to the raising of envelopes to the cued shouts of acclamation. Fear of not doing what everyone else is doing when the Holy Spirit asks me to do something else. Fear of learning to hear God's voice for myself because I might hear something that goes against what the protocol of the church is. The fear extends right down to the need for it to be subconsciously noted from the pulpit every Sunday that at *this* church it is expected that you dress up and *only* when you are told it is okay is it okay to dress casually. If we appear to have it all together by holding to our protocols, then it will all come together at the end.

Fear's best friend is deception. Deception was peering in through the window from outside and laughing. He laughed and laughed his evil sadistic laugh, and it made me want to vomit. I could hear him through the walls. Fear had morphed into the ceiling, while Deception stayed in his horrific, hellish state of evil spirit embodiment. I was instructed by the Holy Spirit to tell deception his influence was bound in Jesus's name and he had to leave. Instantly, I saw a chain thrown around Deception's neck, and he was jerked back away from the window, hurtling backward until he was out of sight. I was not, however, to speak to Fear, as he was welcomed by the people's actions and speech. We cannot bind things that are welcomed.

During the final song, the Lord's presence became so strong that I couldn't stand up. The Holy Spirit quickly instructed me to get on my knees and pay homage to the King. Give Him His due reverence and honor. I then moved into Holy Spirit-initiated intercession, begging for reverence to come to the congregation, for an awareness to be felt in our tangible bodies of the presence of the King in the room. As I rocked and shook and my head swung violently back and forth in the presence of the Almighty King, the pastor got up and spoke of a YouTube video that he had seen. It talked about a band who were telling their stories of traveling to Africa and how in the church services, when they would enter, the congregation would be on their knees and their bodies would be shaking violently and they would be weeping uncontrollably in the presence of God. And how it was something to be desired. But no invitation was given for the Lord to come and have His way with our bodies to teach us how to recognize His presence. Nothing.

As the worship service ended on cue and the service moved into greeting time, I was unable to move, frozen on the floor on my knees between the chair rows. I heard an enormous roar that blew me backward against the chair behind me. As my physical eyes remained closed, I saw the Lion of the Tribe of Judah strongly patrolling back and forth across the front of the sanctuary. My Lord Jesus came in a lion form. It took Him only five or six steps to cross the entire span of the room. His fur was dark golden and his mane like spun golden silk. It flowed as if royal fans were blowing on Him. He shone like the sun. The glow on the floor around Him and on the wall behind Him was blinding. He would walk across the room and then turn and slowly and confidently parade back across. He would stop in the middle of the room and *roar* so loudly that my physical hair literally blew back from my head as the power of his breath hit me. It blew the hair on arms! I heard it with my physical ears. It was deafening. But in all the walking around and greeting of one another, no one else that I could see had heard Him. No one was listening. We had spent the past forty minutes worshipping in our own pre-written, pre-chosen song way and asking Him to come, but when He came, no one greeted Him. No one paid attention. He was invited as the guest of honor, but when He came, He was ignored. Because the protocol for that timeframe of the agenda said that we were supposed to be greeting one another, that is what was done.

I then saw the Holy Spirit. He stood at the front of the pulpit. He took on a man's form, although more majestic and radiant than any royal ever seen. He was dressed in gentleman's clothing. Fine, fine gentleman's clothing. He walked here and there, to this one and then that one, holding out His hand to be shaken, but no one shook His hand back. No one even noticed He was there. I called to Him and asked Him to come to me. He came running! We leapt into each other's arms in my mind's eye, and my spirit woman began to dance with Him. And as I knew He was always in me and had never left, He needed me to see what was happening in the spirit realm. That when we ask the Lord Jesus to be our King and Redeemer and we dedicate our lives to Father God, then the Holy Spirit comes and dwells within us. However, if we ignore Him, then He becomes like the gentleman at the front. The gentleman whom everyone talks about and declares they know and want to lead them, but really, he is just an icon. A cardboard cutout. A religious image that is spoken of in Christian circles to try to define us as a more distinguished and more advanced form of Christians because we speak of Him.

As the greeting time of the agenda came to a conclusion, my Lion took His rightful place on the pulpit. He slowly and regally climbed the stairs of the platform to His rightful place on the pulpit. He sat in all His royal splendor and looked out at the congregation. But as the pastor got up to speak, I saw my Lion get smaller and smaller. Then the pastor hip-checked Him off the stage into the corner, and suddenly He became a stuffed animal. I looked at him, and although the form was that of a stuffed animal, His eyes were still fully real. As our glance met, tears ran down his face and soaked his fur. And then he was gone.

Follow or Die

We have heard prophets for the past two thousand years speak out that Jesus is coming. In my thirteen years as a born-again Christian, I have heard the main international prophets speak their new year's prophecies that the Lord is coming, we have to step it up, and the church has to wake up—*He's coming!* But in the past year, I have seen movement of the Holy Spirit and felt the tangible presence of my God like never before. I have heard countless stories of friends and strangers who can no longer be under the containment of church tradition, rules, theology, and protocol, but must, with no choice, break out and move on when their cries for freedom fall on deaf ears. Their spirit men will be crushed under man's hand if they don't follow the leading of the precious Holy Spirit. The intensity with which I feel the presence of God, the loudness of His voice, and the heaviness of His hand directing me are more real than the skin I wear. And so it is for many, many others. Why now? What's happening? Are we out of time? Is the Word really real? Is the end here?

Stories of Some Who Have Chosen to Get Out of Their Own Way to Allow Jesus to Be Their Way

One set of friends have been studying the spiritual roots of healing for the past several years diligently. The church they were in was moving in the direction of healing ministry. But when it came time for change, time for different, time for new thought patterns, new ways of doing things, new openness to allowing the Holy Spirit to do what *He* wants, the doors closed. But my friends knew they couldn't contain what the Lord had given them, and they moved on. And now He has opened an incredible door of opportunity for them in their new church. The healing mantle has been placed on that house of worship, and the Holy Spirit is drawing believers and non-believers alike to His sweet presence and Glory. They couldn't be contained; the Holy Spirit couldn't be contained in them. They knew they would die if they didn't break out and grow the "talent" that they have been given. They have found their freedom in Him. Where the Spirit of the Lord is, there is freedom.

We have the incredible privilege and honor of being friends with an awesome group of teenagers. Teens who love God more than anyone I have ever known. They have raw, childlike faith. They believe the Word front to back. When God tells them to pray for healing for another, they do it. When the Holy Spirit leads them to worship, they do it. I received an e-mail from one of them. She told me how Daddy continues to give her incredibly prophetic dreams. She stated that she and a few others have been going to a new church, as God's tangible presence is there. She is addicted. She is addicted to the golden rain of our Lord. She is enamored by His beauty. And no one is going to tell her that she cannot go to where He is. She wants to be in His house. She wants to worship with freedom to sing out her heart's song without someone telling her that singing time is over. She's in love. And no one will tell her how she is supposed to love. Freedom.

I know an incredible woman whose love for Jesus shines off her face. She constantly, in every conversation, random or planned, talks of her precious Savior. She is so in love with Jesus. But she was shrouded in unbelief of the King's love for her. Unbelief that had festered and grown over years of hurt and disappointment. But she knew her God could break it, and after years of her crying out, He did. She cried, He heard, and I watched her walk into a leadership meeting and blow us out of the water with her authority and power. She opened her mouth, and the Holy Spirit moved through her to blast us all about unbelief and lack of faith and that the time is *now* to *believe! Just believe!* She didn't care that she sat in a group of women who were twice her age. She didn't care that what she had to say didn't really line up with the theology they held so dear. All she wanted to do was let God be glorified. And that she did.

Another friend fell in love—in full-blown, I-cannot-get-enough-of-you love—with Jesus a few years ago. Her love for Him was uncontainable. At the time, she was one of the worship singers in the church band and led a women's Bible study group. She began to allow the Holy Spirit to tell her what she was to teach at the study. She began to allow Him to move through her body during Sunday worship with hands raised and tears streaming. However, her newfound permission to allow her King to have His way did not fit into the mold of the way things were done. She was asked to contain her emotions when singing. She was asked to step down from leading the Bible study. At which point she said, "No more. No more will any human tell me I cannot speak of the wonders of my King to those in my circle of influence! No more will I contain the power of God in my body when He moves me to tears or to cry out in adoration to Him! No more." She left the mold and moved to where there is none. And now she shines. When she walks into the room, you see Jesus before you see her. When she opens her mouth, you smell God's sweet fragrance before you hear her words. Freedom reigns in that place.

Our favorite church in Stratford is like nothing you have ever seen before. Or maybe you have. The pastor loves Jesus. He loves Him, lives for Him, and would gladly die for Him if the time came for that. He wants nothing more than to allow Holy Spirit to have His way each and every Sunday. Months ago, God told him that church as we knew it was over. "Get out of the way. Throw out your format and ideals. The Holy Spirit will be the new pastor and worship leader, and you will be the MC." And that is precisely what is done. The pastor MCs. The Holy Spirit is the leader. Every week is different. And nothing is planned. The band doesn't prepare songs that they think we should sing. They play as our worship leader Holy Spirit conducts them to. They sing as the Great *I Am* puts words in their mouths. The pastor MCs. Then he gets out of the way. Some days, we will be there in a large circle for two hours, soaking in His presence and praying for one another, before an instrument is lifted. Sometimes, the band is playing before "official start time" even begins, and then three hours later, the band is still playing. There is no human design, no human interference. It is totally God's show, God's plan, and God's order for the day. And in that, the most incredible things happen in the spirit realm. God is moving, and we are following.

I sat with the main leader of a children's ministry here in our city. An incredible ministry that has introduced hundreds of children to their sweet friend Jesus over the past many years. A ministry that is held so dear by many, a ministry that God's hand has been upon since its inception. But in that length of time of doing, complacency has crept in of maintenance. As this leader and I spoke, it became evident that she too felt the tired drain of maintenance, the drain that sucks the life out of passion and vision. Discussion revealed what the Holy Spirit had been trying to break over the past few months. That it was now to be His plan and His way of doing things. Not that the old was wrong. It wasn't. But the time of God's coming is tidal-waving toward us. It is not coming; it is not creeping; it is a freight train heading straight for us, and most don't even see it. It means we are out of time to do things the way we are used to doing them. It is God's turn to, step by step, moment by moment, tell us what to do, when to do it, how to do it. The degree of timing is more crucial than it has ever been at any time in history. That one night at the girls' club, the Holy Spirit told me to read out loud Psalm 97, right *now*. I didn't. I waited because I was enjoying what was happening around me and thought it could wait. But He couldn't. He said it had to be right now. So he asked one of the tweens to do it instead. Why? Because something was brewing. Something was happening in the spirit realm that needed the obedience of a human to speak out God's Word over it, *right at that moment in time.*

There is no more time to do things the way we want. *He* knows what needs to be done, right now, right at this place, at this moment. What He needs are obedient lovers who will say, "Jesus, I don't care if I sing one song or ten this morning; if you need my voice in worship to push back the darkness for the next four hours over this place, I will do it." "Jesus, I don't care if I want to sit comfortably and listen to someone else spoon-feed me revelation that I should be seeking you directly for anyhow; if you want me to get up and do something else right at this moment, I will." We need to get out of the way and do what He wants to do, and *needs* to do.

The Glory of the Lord is waiting to fall on the people called by His name. He has His gates positioned. He has His gatekeepers on standby, waiting for the wave of His commanding hand to open them. "Enter the gates with praise, His courts with thanksgiving." It is when we lay down our well-intentioned, well-planned-out agendas and expend our efforts in thanksgiving and praise that the gates of heaven will be opened and the Glory of the Lord will pour out until there is no more want. When we surrender our well-worn road, most traveled way of doing things, then, and only then, will the Holy Spirit come in His full strength and power and move through our obedient bodies to bring the kingdom of God to earth.

Not knowing what to do is not a comfortable place for an adult to be. Not knowing what the schedule is makes most adults squirm. But it is only when we get to the place of being comfortable in not knowing the agenda that He reveals it to us—step by step, play by play. *That* is when the unknown becomes the high.

The Praises of Creation

My husband has many times commented that I have the hearing of a canine. I can hear the most ridiculous little noise in the midst of chaos. The things that others have to strain to hear and can barely make out, I hear instantly as if they were right behind me. The most quiet but sharp sounds hurt my ears. Treble turned up is excruciating. The screech of my children's iPods causes great pain, and the sound of fingernails on a chalkboard induces vomit. But sometimes, sometimes I hear things that others cannot—things that I know one hundred percent are supernatural.

My hearing has always been very good, but since being born again, the sense has been intensely heightened. Within the past few years, I have heard things around me that I knew were angels speaking or singing. Their sound is intensely high-pitched. What I hear is muffled but clear at the same time. Words that I don't understand, but a language for sure. I didn't tell anyone, just noted the sounds to myself. And as the years have passed, I hear it more and more. I turn to see where my ears are leading me, but I don't see anything with my physical eyes. But I sense their presence. I know they are there.

A visitor came to church one day and brought a CD of something most amazing. It was a CD of a young man from her church in Georgia; when he played his instruments, angels would play theirs in harmony. When he sang, angels would sing backup. And when that CD was played for us, I heard the sound that I had been hearing for the past several years but couldn't speak of to others. I heard confirmation that I was *hearing* angels. Their sound is like no other. Incredibly high-pitched, but stunningly beautiful. Melodic, glorious, deep. In the midst of the highest range of sound is a depth of sound indescribable. It was in that moment of time that Sunday morning that I knew I wasn't crazy, and that I knew I had been given a gift to cherish and nurture.

I hear more and more. One morning at four o'clock as I lay on the couch and reveled in the glorious beauty of my God's love, He let me hear it. Hear the sounds of creation singing out His praises. Hear the melodious chaos of every star, planet, rock, angel, human heart, *every created being that knows Him*—I heard their songs of praise! It was as if I was standing in a stadium before the conference began, where every voice was speaking. Where you can hear the one beside you, but if you change your listening stance, all you can hear is the overall joint noise of the place. That is what I heard. Voices everywhere, but united as one, each singing or speaking a different thing, but together one collection of praise to Him. I heard it. I heard it as clearly as I hear my children call my name. As clearly as I hear the traffic rumbling past on the nearby highway. I heard it. And I was awestruck.

All the time, we read in the Word that "If man doesn't speak it, the rocks will cry out to Him." I have always read that as figurative. Meaning, "Humans, speak up!" But now I am under the conviction that the rocks do cry out His praises. It is beyond our comprehension to think that nature has a voice. That the trees and the flowers and the rocks speak God's praise. Is it possible to stretch our imagination, the blackboard in our brains for the Holy One to illustrate heaven on—that we could possibly believe that *every* created thing is capable of praising Him? I was once at a meeting where an amazing woman of God was speaking. She had the incredible privilege of being taken to heaven on a regular basis for His purposes. She shared with us some of the awesome things that she had seen in heaven, including the praises of creation. She explained that as you walk by, the flowers turn and follow you with their heads. Flowers on earth today follow the sunlight as it moves across the noonday sky. Flowers in heaven follow the inhabitants of heaven as they walk by, as they carry the "Son's" light. The flowers sing. They sing the praises of the Almighty Creator. All the time. The singing and the praises never cease. In children's cartoons, particularly shows targeted at little girls, the colors are vibrant; the flowers and houses and trees sing and talk. Is it possible that the imagination that birthed these shows was incited to do so from the depths of the creator's spirit man, who knows in his innermost being that creation is capable of singing forth praise, and does so? Is it possible that in the recesses of our minds, we remember heaven from whence we came, and it spills forth in this realm as "vivid imagination"?

Tonight, as I step into my secret garden with my God, as I lie down in the quiet to be with Him, He allows me to hear what the rest of creation already knows: the sounds of eternity singing forth His praises. Can you hear it?

Black and white faith is choosing to believe in a God who is very much alive. Choosing to allow Him to guide my life in a wonderful and magnificient way, one that to others may look very bizarre, but to me the follower, a life that will explode with excitement, blessings to self and blessings to others. Did my neat, tidy, skirt-length-below-the-knees upbringing raise me for this kind of out of the box living? Absolutely not. "Follow the rules, attend the building when told, do this, wear that, and you'll be saved." That's what I learned. But the real Jesus showed me the real truth. That He is not neat and tidy. He is not "blend into the crowd and don't stand out." And He definitely is not "stick to the human's rules and do as you're told." He is black and white. He is "here's an opportunity for a miracle let's do this!" He is, "what the Father in Heaven says, I do." And He asks us to be that too. Follow His lead, serve others, share His love, enter eternity hearing the words "well done good and faithful one." Black and white. It's so much better than the gray.

Printed in the United States
by Bookmasters

Printed in the United States
By Bookmasters